YOU'RE NOT TOAST.

5 Counter-Intuitive Steps to Ditch Burnout & Revive Your Rock-Star Self

SCOTT ANDERSON

You're Not Toast: 5 Counter-Intuitive Steps to Ditch Burnout &
Revive Your Rock-Star Self

For Sheila.

For everything.

Forever.

Contents

Introduction

HOPE

As we embark on our journey together, there's a fundamental truth I need you to hear: no matter how burned out you feel, no matter how many things you have tried that have failed, crashed, and burned, there is *hope*. In fact, it's the driving force behind my decision to write this book.

This book exists for three reasons:

- To convince every overachiever, striver, and perfectionist trapped in burnout that there is a way out.

- To show that it's not only possible to get beyond burnout, but it's also possible to start living a life that may seem unimaginable today.

- To share the techniques you need to break out of burnout, reclaim your energy, and get your life back. When done consistently, these techniques deliver more than a temporary fix—they offer permanent freedom from burnout.

There is hope. You're not toast.

Most people I've encountered who are experiencing burnout, including myself, have two things in common:

1. They've been overachievers their entire lives. Straight A's in school chasing that next degree. Starting a business (or businesses). Trying to achieve the C-suite. Becoming a partner at a law firm. Whatever it was they strove for, over time, achievement grew to carry a toxic importance in their life, which I'll explain more later.

2. They're perfectionists, but this is a special kind of perfectionism. No matter how perfect their performance is, it's never quite perfect enough for their own satisfaction.

The third trait I'll add is that most people in prime burnout share the desire to take on more and more, and this is where toxic achievement comes into play. Their lust for achievement compels them to heap more onto an already full plate because they lack the ability to set boundaries. In fact, they're almost pathologically incapable of saying "no."

Is any of this familiar?

If so, my clients are no different from you—nor am I. Most of us have been setting super-high standards for performance all of our lives. And if we're being honest here, in some ways, it served us well. The perfectionism, the willingness to run toward the professional fire, the rolling up of sleeves to solve hard problems, and the willingness to say "yes" when others say "no," have made you the go-to person in every arena of your life. That's because it's become a part of your professional brand.

Let me ask you, how's it working for you? It's not. Here's the BIG problem: It's killing you—and that's probably the reason you're reading this book.

After decades of working with people experiencing burnout, I've found that of all the obstacles, this toxic "professional brand" is the hardest to face and the hardest to change. Why? How can you suddenly stop doing the things that have always worked for you (until they didn't)?

But when you're in it, I mean deep in burnout, you can't see that the very drive to achieve—the compulsion to excel—has, in essence, become your kryptonite. Instead of helping you achieve, it becomes your nemesis. I say this from personal experience. The very things that had propelled me, not only in my career, but in every area of my life, had become my undoing. Back in the heyday of the dot-com boom, with 22 employees depending on me, my "superpowers" failed. I found myself deep in a burnout spiral, and I realized, a little bit too late, that I didn't have a plan B.

I describe it as my *Groundhog Day* moment. I felt like I was starring in my own movie, lying in bed hearing the alarm go off at 6:00 AM as Sonny and Cher's "I Got You Babe" blared from the clock radio. I'm thinking I don't know if I can do this one more time.

I didn't know if I could get up another day more exhausted than when I went to bed the night before. But I knew that I didn't have a choice but to get up anyway because there was no one else to do my work for me. I wasn't sure I could put on another happy face and head out one more time to earn a living by pushing through and working harder.

What I didn't know at the time was that I had a choice to do it another way. I didn't know there was hope. That there was life beyond burnout.

I'm here to tell you there is! Everything you need to get free from the hopelessness you may feel, you'll find in Part 2 when I share my *Burnout Breakthrough System*. Have I found a unique solution to the problem of burnout? Honestly, I don't know. But what I do know is that my method works especially well for high-performance leaders, people operating at the highest levels in their careers, their communities, and the world. People like you.

As you read on, I need to be transparent. Beginning this process will not be a walk-in-the-park, snap-your-fingers-once type of thing. In fact, before we begin, you have to recognize and accept three challenges:

- You have to believe there *is* hope and that you're not alone.

- You have to acknowledge that the cause of your distress may well be your burnout symptoms.

- You have to admit (and eventually let go) that everything you've known how to do up to this point, everything that has gotten you to where you are today, may be the very things that are killing you.

If you're anything like me, that last one is the toughest— because how do you let go of and change the exact things that gained you success in the first place? How do you believe that if these things don't work, something else will?

The truth is those "superpowers" served you to a point until they took on a toxicity that is now affecting your life, your health, your business, and the lives of those you care about most. There is another way: the *Burnout Breakthrough System*. There is life after burnout.

For now, you don't even have to believe it will work to get the results. You just have to read on and begin to do the work.

There is hope. You're not toast.

Scott

If you're ready to tackle your number one burnout symptom right now so you get some relief fast, give me and my team a call. Book a call here: fastfixcall.com.

P.S.
We don't practice medicine, and we don't pretend to. Therefore, we highly recommend you see your doctor for a complete physical before you begin implementing the *Burnout Breakthrough System*. A lot of you don't go to the doctor (ever), which is precisely why we're making this recommendation. It's important to first rule out that there are no physical factors—like adrenal or blood sugar issues—that could potentially slow your emergence from burnout.

PART 1

Life After Burnout

I probably don't need to share what I'm about to share—because if you're reading this book, unfortunately, you're already living it. Here are some of the more well-known facts and stats about burnout among working Americans:

Burnout Facts:

1. **Scope**: 76% of employees say they are burned out, and 28% state they suffer burnout very often to always.[1]

2. **Health**: Burnout is directly linked to chronic stress, depression, anxiety, cardiovascular diseases, and higher risk of type 2 diabetes. (Occupational Health Psychology)

3. **Performance and Productivity**: Employees experiencing burnout are 63% more likely to take sick leave and 2.5 times more likely to be actively looking for another job. This lost productivity costs the global economy roughly $322 billion annually.[2]

4. **Work-Life Balance**: 46% of employees cite workload as their primary stressor, and 20% cite balancing work and their personal lives.[3]

---

1 https://www.gallup.com/workplace/288539/employee-burnout-biggest-myth.aspx
2 https://www.gallup.com/workplace/288539/employee-burnout-biggest-myth.aspx
3 https://www.apa.org/topics/healthy-workplaces/workplace-burnout

5. **Burnout and Remote Work:** Remote workers often struggle with work-home boundaries and the ability to switch off, resulting in overwork and exhaustion.[4]

6. **Employee Retention:** 52% of employees cite burnout as the reason for leaving their jobs[5]

7. **Long Hours:** Americans work on average 1,786 hours per year, which is higher than most developed countries.[6]

8. **Mental Health Crisis:** Burnout is closely related to mental health. Eighty-three percent of employees feel emotionally drained from their work, a key symptom of burnout.[7]

Finally, stress is deadly. The six leading causes of death, from heart disease to cancer and suicide, can be caused, or made more acute, by stress. As you read on, keep in mind that my goal in this book is to find healthy and sustainable ways to neutralize your stress before it neutralizes you. So, let's begin.

---

4 https://pmc.ncbi.nlm.nih.gov/articles/PMC10267312/

5 https://www.shrm.org/topics-tools/news/inclusion-diversity/burnout-shrm-research-2024

6 https://www.oecd.org/en/data/indicators/hours-worked.html

7 https://mhanational.org/sites/default/files/Mind%20the%20Workplace%20-%20MHA%20Workplace%20Health%20Survey%202021%202.12.21.pdf

CHAPTER 1

Beyond What You Believe Possible

When you're in burnout, when things seem hopeless, and you feel powerless to change them, a new reality can seem nearly impossible and too good to imagine. Believe me when I say, there is a way to move beyond your burnout state to a place of satisfaction and possibility in your life that is better than you've ever experienced. It's waiting for you if you're willing to do the work.

The best way to show you what is possible is to have you meet some of my clients who, like you, felt stuck. But by doing the work, each one found light at the end of the burnout tunnel (and no, it wasn't an oncoming train). Each one discovered burnout isn't a terminal condition; it's something that can not only be treated but cured—permanently.

Their stories are proof positive that beyond burnout lies a life in which you, your career, and your relationships thrive. A life of possibility beyond what you've imagined.

Michael: Out of Gas

Michael is an engineer in the energy sector who worked grueling hours meeting high-level demands. When he came to me, he was so burned out that he'd requested a 90-day sabbatical. His request was striking because Michael is a tough cookie, he's no quitter, and he's been serving in an industry that's been a bit precarious for the last 10 years.

For Michael, taking "time off" felt completely counterintuitive. For a decade, he'd faithfully led his firm's relationship with its most critical partner. For this guy who always runs toward the fire in any crisis to now ask for a sabbatical indicated to me, and to him, that his pain was overwhelming. No one in his generation believes they're entitled to "time off." The very idea went against everything he is. His request scared both him and his wife.

But Michael realized he couldn't do it a day longer. For months, he'd woken up completely exhausted and depleted. He knew that if he kept pushing, one day, he wasn't going to be able to answer the bell, and calling in sick indefinitely wasn't an option.

Two weeks into using the *Burnout Breakthrough System*, he shared his worst-case scenario fears: if this 90-day sabbatical didn't make him feel better, how could he go back to work? As the breadwinner, how could he support his family? But he followed this by saying that for the first time in a long time, he experienced hope, giving him the belief that there is a way through this—not only to return to work but to reclaim his life.

In those early weeks, Michael learned to recognize his burnout symptoms and see them not as a death sentence without a cure but as something that could be treated and healed. He saw he wasn't alone in his struggle. Through implementing the R&R Technique, which I will dive deep into in Chapter 4, he quickly felt relief—proving there was a way out of burnout. He'd tried different things before, but seeing the early results was what gave him hope and was the critical difference that kept him going.

Michael learned the techniques he needed to regain the energy to not only return to work but to work at a higher level and support his family in ways he hadn't imagined before.

Ethan: The Former Workaholic

Ethan was the poster child for the overachiever who believed that working harder, pushing harder, and clocking 50-60 hour workweeks for months on end was the only way to success. These hard-to-let-go-of tactics had gotten him this far until the weight of it all came down hard—in exhaustion and negativity in every area of his life. He didn't know there was another way. He didn't realize there was hope.

Now, Ethan is my poster child of a fully recovered, burned-out workaholic. Even though it felt completely foreign and counterintuitive, we reduced his workweek to 20 hours. To Ethan's surprise, in a few weeks time, his burnout symptoms disappeared and haven't returned. Ethan will tell you he's living his best life and enjoying every day more fully than he did prior to his burnout. Today, his business is thriving and performing at a higher level largely because he let go of his workaholic lifestyle and refused to wear its badge of honor another day.

Like Ethan, most of us learned to:

- Work harder.
- Worry more.

This leaves only two levers available for us to pull when the chips are down. We think the solution to our burnout is to work harder, strive harder, and worry more because that's what used to work. Now, for reasons that seem opaque to us at the moment, they don't. But with those as our go-to tools, we have no plan B.

That's why I created the plan B I want to share with you in Part 2.

Brandi: A Matter of Life and Health

After suffering decades of chronic burnout, I met Brandi with a doctor's urgent warning that if she didn't make changes, she could do permanent damage to her health. Despite her warning, she continued to lean into her entrepreneur "superpowers" of persistence and tenacity long after they'd become her kryptonite. By the time she found me, Brandi had reached a point of no return—ready to sell her business and just get out.

Thirty days into the *Burnout Breakthrough System*, her burnout symptoms virtually vanished, which was fantastic because my biggest fear for Brandi was that selling her business and simply walking away might further harm her health.

Shutting her business down would not have resolved her burnout symptoms; it would have left her with nothing to do—a dangerous thing for us overachievers. What seems logical to relieve burnout actually can make it worse. The typical answer is to double down and fix the problem—if it's the cash flow, if it's the profit margin, work harder even if it's slowly killing you mentally, physically, and even spiritually, like it was for Brandi.

By implementing the techniques from the *Burnout Breakthrough System*, Brandi's symptoms improved so much that she went against her doctor's advice to shut down her business and, instead, started another one.

After many years of working with clients just like Brandi, I've seen over and over again that shutting it all down or taking a sabbatical won't cure burnout—the only way to ensure your relief will be long-lasting is to address the underlying causes.

It's a cruel trick burnout plays on us. But doubling down, using the familiar go-to tactics that have become your kryptonite, begins to slowly kill you mentally, physically, and spiritually in your loss of hope. Even if it feels counterintuitive, if you want permanent relief from your burnout symptoms, deal with the underlying causes.

The Paradox of Fix or Avoid

In the clutches of burnout, both Brandi and Michael got fooled by burnout's paradox. It's why countless people will try anything to fix or avoid their *symptoms*:

- Taking a vacation or even just a weekend away—only to find that when they return, nothing has changed.

- Divorcing their spouse, thinking the relationship and stress at home is the problem.

- Going on a sabbatical, again, is a short-term bandaid, not a long-term solution.

The paradox of fix or avoid is that what feels intuitive or logical won't work. But that overachiever mindset tells us that doing nothing is not an option either. And we get confused when what worked before doesn't anymore, and our fight-or-flight instinct comes in—to fight and fix it, or take flight and avoid the symptoms.

The answer, as we'll discuss in Chapter 3, is to adopt a peaceful attitude toward the disturbing emotions that trigger your fight-or-flight.

Burnout's Quicksand

Dr. Harris, who advocates Acceptance and Commitment Therapy, first introduced me to quicksand as a metaphor for burnout. Whether you're human or an animal, when you fall into it, your instinct is to struggle, which only makes the situation worse by sucking you deeper into it. Again, it's counterintuitive that your natural instinct to fight actually kills you faster. Burnout is no different.

The trouble is, doing nothing won't prevent you from being sucked down into the quicksand—it will just take a little longer. The same applies to burnout; you can't fix it or avoid it. The real way to fix quicksand is to lie back and try to float on the sand. Doing this distributes your body weight evenly across the surface, relieving the pressure pulling you downward and allowing you to slowly paddle your way out.

As Michael and Brandi discovered, the same concept applies to burnout. You can't fix or avoid your way out of it. You need to adopt a peaceful attitude to uncover the root causes and develop a strategy that works to get you out.

Caught in quicksand or burnout, changing your natural, instinctual way of doing things is the only solution.

Mastering Your Joystick

Another metaphor I like is from Chuck Yeager. Besides being the first pilot to exceed the speed of sound, he's also known for saving thousands of pilots' lives, figuring out how to correct an aircraft in a tailspin: **pull down on the joystick,** the lever that controls the plane, to get the nose up and out of the spin. But that makes no sense when you're hurtling toward Earth at 400 miles an hour. Your knee-jerk reaction would be the complete opposite—to pull up, which unfortunately doesn't work. Through personal experience, Yeager discovered that acting counterintuitively—by pulling down on the joystick—corrected the spin and saved his life.

He taught this unfamiliar, unnatural tactic to other fighter pilots, saving many lives.

Both metaphors—the quicksand and the joystick— demonstrate that the only way to save yourself from burnout and pull yourself out of its tailspin is to act against your instincts.

CHAPTER 2

Freedom from Burnout

If you're reading this book, you may be in a place of burnout that feels hopeless because you've exhausted all ideas about how to get out. The good news, as I said before, is that you don't have to believe that the techniques I describe will work. You just have to do them.

Years ago, when I was deep in burnout, I began this work with a complete lack of faith. At a point of desperation, I read the work of Christina Maslach, a brilliant psychologist at the University of California, Berkeley, whose research focused on occupational burnout. Using some of the ideas from her work, I slowly began to create effective tools to address my symptoms. If something didn't work, I tried something else.

Things began to come together, but only after a lot of painful trial and error.

Night and Day

At 58, I walked away from the ad agency I had founded.

Remember my version of Groundhog Day? The endless cycle of exhaustion, of waking up to the same crushing weight, the same relentless demands? I didn't think I could

do it for one more day. But I also believed I had no choice—
because, in my mind, no one else would step up. No one else
could carry the burden. I was caught in the web of my own
toxic overachievement, completely unable to see another
way.

All I wanted—my only wish—was that I had enough energy
left to pull myself out of bed one more time... to face one
more day.

Shortly after I left the agency, I began coaching and offering
mental health therapy to executives. It was then that I was
struck by the irony of my situation—I had left the agency
without ever doing the work required to address the root
causes of my own burnout symptoms. After a session with
an orthodontist named Tom, I experienced a seminal
moment.

Tom described his burnout symptoms as so severe that if
he had to look into one more child's mouth, he might do
something he'd deeply regret. The exhaustion and loss of
hope in his words resonated with me. I shared his feeling
that he'd expended all of his options to get out of burnout. He
felt stuck. The good news? I'd already begun experimenting
with new techniques to relieve my own symptoms beyond
an external fix like yoga or meditation.

I admit that early in my work with Tom, it felt a bit like the
blind leading the blind. Then, as I began to share some of
the practices I was using to deal with my own symptoms,
they seemed to help him, too. We started with the Rest
and Release technique, which I've mentioned before. It's an

adaptation of a practice Michael Singer shares in his book *Untethered Soul.* As Tom implemented the R&R technique in his life, his symptoms seemed to improve.

Cautiously hopeful, I began to think bigger. If this worked for Tom and me, could it work for others? Either way, Tom's positive results suggested a way forward. Gradually, we expanded the R&R technique into group therapy. It started in the basement of my tiny office with six people, including myself, who all suffered from severe burnout and were searching for a way out.

The group therapy proved to be a success. The participants began to see improvements in the lessening of their symptoms. As they felt better, free from exhaustion, and with a newfound sense of hope, the group expanded. We then added a virtual component on Zoom for people who lived out of state. With the expansion and ongoing positive results, I began to think we really had something. One of the most important discoveries was the power of the group because people were able to see that they weren't alone in their burnout, even if their symptoms were very specific to them.

I continued to experiment and work with new techniques from Maslach's research on dealing with burnout, exhaustion, anxiety, and depression. By adapting certain practices, I eventually codified a process with the goal of making it as practical and pragmatic as possible.

Later in the book, we will talk more about a diagnostic tool I created called the Beyond Burnout Assessment, a set of questions based on the Maslach Burnout Inventory (MCI). The results are intended to give you an idea of the degree of burnout from which you're suffering. When I took the assessment myself, I was surprised by my results. Resentment and victimization turned out to be two hallmarks of my burnout. It didn't make sense to me at the time, but as I moved through my recovery, I understood that I had convinced myself that other people were responsible for my life's downturn. So much so that it felt like every bad luck break I experienced was because the world was against me.

- My marriage was hanging by a thread, and my child was struggling with substance abuse and mental health—both deeply affected by my absence and lack of presence in our family.

- The fear in my wife's eyes as I jumped headfirst into a new coaching business—armed with nothing but a Master's degree in counseling and no safety net.

- And then, my darkest moment—the one that shattered me completely: The death of my son from an overdose.

Today, when I look at this list, I realize how close I came to losing everything that mattered to me. At the same time, it was also a gift because it gave me the motivation to search for a solution to escape from burnout, even one that, as discussed, felt foreign and against every instinct in my body.

Ironically, it was this counterintuitiveness that gave me hope—the possibility that maybe everything I had previously believed to work in my life was wrong. It's similar to the

Seinfeld episode when George Costanza gets fired from the Yankees. At some point in the episode, George realizes that everything he tried to do "to play the game" actually hurt him and instead landed him with no job. In the same way, I began to ask the question, *If everything I did before wasn't working, why don't I try something new?*

With continued trial and error, the techniques I gathered and adapted eventually became the foundation of the *Burnout Breakthrough System*, which has now helped hundreds of people reclaim their lives and permanently shut the door on burnout.

Right now, you might be thinking, *okay, Scott, this sounds great for other people, but how do I know it will work for me?*

It's a fair question, but one I hope I can answer by sharing the signs of recovery my clients typically see in the first 15-20 days into their recovery.

- **Recovery of Energy**: Exhaustion is like the canary in the coal mine—it's the symptom people typically feel first that tells them there's cause for concern. However, reclaiming physical and mental energy is also the first signal that clients are getting better.

- **Renewed Confidence**: In the next phase of recovery, my clients begin to work on intrusive and painful thoughts (called DTEs—disturbing thoughts and emotions). They begin to identify and eliminate the running tape of negative and defeating thoughts in their mind—and replace them with more positive thoughts. The result is a return in their confidence and sense of hope.

- **Mindset Shift from Negative to Positive:** As you'll see in Part 2, clients' negative thoughts are replaced with newly identified values that are meaningful to them—and they become their new true North—a new sort of mental Guiding Principles System, or GPS. With this in place, suddenly, life becomes more enjoyable and fulfilling and delivers their desired outcomes.

- **Restored Connection:** Often, clients are unaware of the isolation burnout creates. Their renewed connection with people they care about can be startling but wonderful.

- **Living a Life That Is Better Than Ever:** We call this phase "Beyond Burnout." This is when the exhaustion has completely disappeared, and clients are living a life they didn't know was possible. For the first time in a long time, they begin to ask, "What else is possible for me—in my relationships, my career, and my growth in mind, body, and spirit?"

This process isn't magic, but when you do the work, you, too, can experience the same results as those I just described. In Part 2, you'll discover practical tools to reclaim your life. The techniques and strategies in my Burnout Breakthrough System are battle-tested and proven to work.

Your job is to simply put them into action in your life.

Before we go any further, I've developed the following *Quick Checklist for Burnout* to assess the severity of your symptoms. Go through all seven statements. Score yourself on a scale from 1 to 5. 1 being this is not me at all—never. And 5 being—this is me—always.

Be honest with yourself, answer truthfully, and your results will reveal your starting point to freedom from burnout. (Note: this is a concise version of my formal online Beyond Burnout Assessment I mentioned earlier that I've included in the resource section at the back of the book.)

Questions (Scale 1-5: 1 = "Never," 5 = "Always")

- I feel exhausted, even after a good night's sleep.
- I have negative thoughts about my job.
- I am easily irritated by small problems or by others at work.
- I feel unappreciated or misunderstood by my co-workers.
- I feel under constant pressure to succeed.
- I feel that there is more work than I can reasonably handle.
- I feel that I am achieving less than I should or not getting what I want from my job.

Scoring Guidelines (Total Possible: 7 to 35)

- **7-11:** You have no signs of burnout.
- **12-18:** You suffer a few signs of burnout.
- **19-24:** You are at risk of falling into burnout.
- **25-30:** It's likely you are at a severe risk of burnout.

- **31-35:** Most likely, you're suffering symptoms of severe burnout.

Whatever your results are, I already know you're in the right place. There is a way out, so let's continue.

CHAPTER 3
Clearing Your Hurdles

Burned-out people are, by definition, good at overcoming obstacles. Unfortunately, burnout is not a 3D object you can see, approach, and clear, like the hurdles that Australian athlete Shirley Strickland soared over with ease at the 1952 Helsinki Olympic Games. Shirley cleared eight hurdles in 10.9 seconds to win her first Olympic gold and set a new world record.

Unlike a hurdle that can be seen, approached, and cleared, burnout isn't tangible. At its core, it's a constellation of DTEs, or disruptive thoughts and emotions, and trying to "fix" them on your own often worsens your burnout.

In this chapter, I want to walk through the seven most common challenges people face in trying to get to the other side of burnout—freedom.

The Seven Most Common Hurdles:

1. **"It's not me—it's everyone else."**

    In burnout, we become convinced that the root of the problem lies outside of us. It's something external like our job, our boss, our coworkers, our spouse, our kids, our parents and siblings—even our next-door neighbor. But nothing could be further from the truth, because *burnout is an inside job.* We are the cause of our own burnout. We have to look in the mirror and admit that we are the problem. But if we are causing the burnout, then we also have the power to escape from it.

My *Burnout Breakthrough System* will help you identify the untruths your DTEs are telling you so you can recognize that you are creating your own burnout. My system will put you in the driver's seat to freedom. *You* can change you—and in part 2, you'll learn how.

2. **"I've lost my superpowers."**

The irony in this statement is that your superpowers are exactly what got you into burnout in the first place. They created the toxic overachievement we described earlier—your kryptonite.

- Being overly responsible
- Always taking the lead and running *into* the professional fire
- Setting crazy high standards for performance (aka perfectionism)

Suddenly, when these powers begin to fail, we feel like a comic book hero stripped of our superhuman strength to fight off the forces of evil. The go-to tactics we've relied on, like pulling all-nighters, working through weekends, and taking on more and more so we're indispensable at home, at work, and in our community—no longer work. However, it's all we know how to do. When you take away those superpowers, we question who we are without them.

Here's the truth. You still have the same unique abilities and strengths. But year after year, the physical and mental toll they take on you increases. As you build your career, you continue to set the bar higher and higher, demanding more of you and your performance. But at what cost? In burnout, at some point, you will eventually hit a wall.

My process helps you recognize that you haven't lost your superpowers; they're just trapped beneath a charred layer of burnout. Your lack of ability isn't the problem. However, the solution is to reframe the unrealistic expectations you've placed on yourself your entire life. We forget that we have built our careers over decades, but the principles and strategies that worked at age 20 don't necessarily work now. Life has changed. Work has changed. Your responsibilities have changed. Your first step toward freedom from burnout is a shift in mindset so you are able to set boundaries and say no. So the demands you take on never become too much to handle. The ability to set boundaries will free you from working 60+-hour weeks. It is possible.

3. **"I've got this—I can fix it myself."**

The truth is you can't. Ironically, the very fact that you're reading this book may mean you're trying to fix burnout on your own. You've come to the right place because *You're Not Toast* offers a unique way to fix your condition, but not the way you may be thinking. You must approach burnout differently than any other problem you've faced in the past. Instead of relying on your own abilities to fix it, you have to invest in a method that will.

I consider myself the ground-zero burnout patient number one, which forced me to design a method that worked and that I believed in. I wanted a solution that was practical, pragmatic, and simple. And I succeeded. My *Burnout Breakthrough* approach to your recovery isn't "mind over matter" (that's what landed you in burnout); it is *matter over mind*, meaning mastering your mind and your thoughts.

4. **The avoidance strategy**

This challenge is the opposite of "I can fix it myself." It's thinking you can run away from burnout. We've already talked about how avoiding your symptoms without discovering what lies beneath them never works. You might have heard this saying before, "No matter where you are, there you are." This statement is true in your burnout.

Remember Michael's request for a sabbatical? That was his attempt to outrun burnout, which didn't turn out well. I worked with another woman from Krakow, Poland, who was also deep in a burnout spiral. But as high achievers will do, even in burnout, she took on more. So, even with her symptoms and the demands of her high-profile job, she took a Ukrainian family into her home that had been displaced by the Russian invasion.

Aware of the severity of her burnout, she also requested a 90-day sabbatical. A few days before the end of her time away, she contacted me. She reported her burnout symptoms had worsened in her time off. In working through my process, she was able to shift her focus to what lay beneath her symptoms. Today she is highly successful at a job she at one time thought she'd have to abandon. She reports that she's happier in her life than she's ever been. She is another example that you can't avoid dealing with your symptoms. You have to do the work to resolve them.

This Band-Aid approach to avoiding burnout is steeped in the culture of the American workplace. How many of us work incredibly hard for 50 weeks a year just so we "earn" the two-week vacation that's supposed to be the magic wand and remedy for burnout? I have news for you—there is no magic wand for avoiding your burnout symptoms. You have to face them, unravel them, and find out what lies beneath them.

5. **Uber-responsibility and perfectionism**

At first glance, being highly responsible seems like an unquestionably good trait. But when we take on more and more, to the point it becomes an unrealistic amount of responsibility, then it becomes a problem. It's not just the disproportionate amount of responsibility—it's our belief that we have to deliver a perfect performance every day without fail, or the world will stop spinning on its axis.

An example is a client I spoke with recently who told me that he is singularly responsible for the company's one customer, who accounts for 50% of the billing. He believes that if he ever lost this account, it would be game over for him, his team, and his family. So he works tremendously long hours and refuses to ever fully unplug from work even when he's home. He feels compelled to be available every day at any time, day or night. He never turns off his phone. Of course, this customer is highly satisfied with the attention they receive, but for my client, it has resulted in severe exhaustion, anxiety, and depression. What eventually happened? Due to health problems, my client was forced to take three months off.

This particular challenge is tough because typically responsible individuals are highly intelligent and able to anticipate outcomes as few others can. Their ability is a huge benefit to them and to their company.

In order to shift your mindset and take steps toward freedom from burnout, you need to unlearn this need to be overly responsible. You have to adjust the work ethic you placed on yourself at age 20. This adjustment can be hard and feel scary because you have been reliant on it for so many years. Believe me, I've been there. However, there is a way to work smarter, work fewer hours, and take on a healthy amount of responsibility. The "how to do this" awaits you in Part 2.

6. The terminal fear

This challenge refers to the paralyzing fear that there is no cure for your burnout. When you are suffering severe symptoms, it is hard to see beyond this narrow viewpoint. When you're trapped in this limited perspective, it can feel like there is no solution— no hope that life can change. It feels like Groundhog Day.

It's not true. If you're in this place, believe that there is a cure. The techniques that you will discover in my *Burnout Breakthrough System* can bring you permanent freedom.

7. The isolation chamber

One of the most debilitating effects of burnout is isolation. Burnout drags its victims into a corner, remote from everything and everyone they care about—ironically, they are the exact things and people that used to make life worth living. It's the terminal fear we just spoke of that keeps you caught in burnout, triggering the isolation that leaves you feeling cut off, lonely, and resentful. What is worse is that you hold the keys to unlock the door of your isolation. But when we're in the burnout spiral, we refuse to open the door and let ourselves out.

You will discover that a natural byproduct of using the techniques I will share is emerging from this profound loneliness. When you implement the Burnout Breakthrough practices, the isolation dissipates. This truth goes back to the importance of working in a group so you can see that you're not alone in your struggle. Through being part of a community, you discover that burnout is a common problem that has a specific solution.

My group started with six people sitting in folding chairs in the basement of my office. Each participant understood that while everyone's burnout is unique to them, there are common tenets to how each of them experienced it. Connecting with a nonjudgmental community will help you take a big step forward in your recovery. This idea of community still plays a major role in my process today.

Before we leave the seven most common hurdles, there's one more dilemma to discuss, and it's one that can be painful. In the burnout spiral, many clients feel that they're asked to make the impossible choice to either succeed at work or to succeed at home—that it's impossible to do both. By the time they reach this choice, they often feel like they're failing at both endeavors.

If you find yourself at this crossroads, I want to tell you—you don't have to make a choice. My clients find that in their recovery, as they clear each hurdle one by one, not only do they find success at both work and at home, but their performance in both places far exceeds what they considered their best days before burnout.

The Beyond Burnout Assessment

It's time to take a deeper look at where you might fall in your burnout. The Beyond Burnout Assessment is the actual diagnostic tool I use with clients. Using this assessment, we discover their starting point before they begin their work using the *Burnout Breakthrough System*. These results allow them to better understand their symptoms and work toward the outcome they want.

Creating my Beyond Burnout Assessment involved the careful process of taking the original 250 questions in the Maslach Burnout Inventory (MCI), which is based on decades of research, and distilling them down to just 25.

As you begin the assessment, these three things will help you:

- **Have an Open Mind**: Do your best to lay aside any fears, misgivings, or doubts you may have. Pay attention to the power of your thoughts, especially when they might tell you that this test won't help you.

- **Be Honest**: Answer each question as honestly as you can. No one will see the results except you—so tell the truth.

- **Don't Try to Ace the Test**: For you overachievers, you can't get an "A" on a self-assessment. Take that thought out of your mind. A perfect score is unattainable.

The assessment's purpose is simple: to help you identify the clinical symptoms of your burnout. No matter how you score, low or high, the fact is, there is a solution. My hope is that as you answer the questions, you will begin to view burnout as a knowable, identifiable, and real problem that can be solved—something that you no longer need to fear.

As previously discussed, to access the online Beyond Burnout Assessment, please find the link in the resource section at the back of the book. It is self-guided and walks you through the questions. Your results will automatically be sent to you. The assessment is completely free, and so are the recommendations that we provide based on your results.

When you're finished taking the assessment, be sure to return to the book so you discover my proven process to emerge from the all-consuming exhaustion and despair of burnout.

CHAPTER 4

The Key to Freedom

When I was burned out, I felt like it was the end of the world—like the exhaustion and the overwhelm consumed every part of me and my life. As previously mentioned, I couldn't see beyond my own perspective. I was stuck. Alone. Hopeless. But I charged on because that's what I knew how to do.

However, this time, I poured my relentless effort into a search for a solution to get out of burnout. I tried everything, and at first, nothing seemed to work. I experimented with talk therapy, yoga, and silent retreats. I even attempted medication—everything short of shock therapy. But nothing came close to relieving my burnout symptoms.

Then I asked myself, *What if I did the opposite of what isn't working? What if I tried something counterintuitive to what I'd been told or taught? What if, instead of trying to swallow my frustration and despair, I actually leaned into those feelings? What if there was a way to sit and be with my disturbing thoughts and emotions instead of running from them?*

Little did I know where the answers to these questions would lead me.

My Sea of Change

This shift in my thinking became a sea of change in me and in my life. The R&R technique was the first key that unlocked the door to let me out of burnout. Practicing this technique lessened my burnout symptoms by 80%. But before I describe the technique itself, I want to share more about my path to its discovery and why it's the first step to your freedom from burnout.

I figured out that in my initial efforts to heal my burnout, I relied on my mind to try to solve the problem. I soon discovered that my mind was actually the bottleneck keeping me stuck in burnout. This realization motivated me to read voraciously about treating burnout from every source I could get my hands on. What I found in my research is that the common denominator to breaking free from burnout is the ability to articulate the emotion you're feeling when you feel it and then identify where that physical sensation is happening in your body.

My Epiphany

When an uncomfortable feeling bubbled up, I started to practice identifying the emotion and then locating where I felt it in my body. If I felt frustrated, I would name that emotion and then identify where I felt it in my body—for example, the pain on the right side of my chest. Then I thought, *What if I took this process a step further and let myself experience the pain as deeply as I could?* I imagined one of those tiny cameras used in heart catheterizations being inserted into my pain.

I was shocked to find that when I let myself get curious about the pain—the frustration—without running away from it, or trying to fix it, something really good happened. The physical pain dissipated. This practice of leaning into the pain and the emotion became the origin of the Relaxation and Release technique, or R&R.

The pain I'd been feeling in my chest was nothing more than trapped energy. Typically, when we experience unpleasant sensations in our body, it triggers "fight-or-flight." But when the danger is just perceived and isn't real—when we are not actually being chased by a sabertooth tiger—it's easy for those feelings of fear, anger, or despair to become trapped. Using the R&R Technique enabled me to minimize and even eliminate the perceived pain in my chest caused by the disturbing emotion.

I learned that I didn't have to fix my disturbing thoughts and emotions; I didn't need to wrestle them to the ground. I simply needed to be curious, notice, and then lean into the pain to release it.

However, there is a paradox in the R&R Technique.

The Paradox of R&R

We've identified that the typical overachiever is taught to charge on, to strive for more—(*and often without success*). When we fall into burnout, we then turn our minds to fixing it. My technique does the opposite.

Here lies the paradox: the solution is not a matter of the mind—it's a matter of the body. The answer lies in your body. Your freedom from burnout is not about trying to figure something out. It's about getting curious and noticing what's going on inside your body when you experience disturbing thoughts and emotions.

If you're shaking your head, ask yourself the same question I did: *What if I did something completely different from what I have been doing that isn't working?* And really, what do you have to lose?

You may have similar questions that you did earlier.

That's great, Scott, that the technique worked for you, but I've tried all kinds of relaxation tools before, and none of them have worked—so why will your R&R Technique work?

The R&R Technique isn't about generalized relaxation like taking a hot bath, getting a massage, or doing breathwork. It's about feeling and locating where in your body that negative energy is trapped—and then allowing it to release. The concept of *allowing* is critical. By allowing the release, you're no longer holding onto something. The "relax" part of the technique is important, but the "release" part is infinitely more so because you're allowing the trapped energy wrapped up in your disturbing thoughts and emotions (DTEs) to leave your body.

Here are the most common questions I hear from clients:

Using the R&R Technique, how long will it take for me to feel relief?

For me, it was immediate because when the physical sensation went away, so did the emotion attached to it—the two things happened in tandem. The relief time can vary, but typically, people will feel significantly better within 10 to 14 days of practicing the R&R Technique.

How long do I have to practice the R&R Technique?

It comes down to consistency, not perfection. I recommend you practice R&R each time disturbing thoughts and emotions come up. Early on, you may not catch them every time, and that's okay. Even if you only notice the DTEs 10% of the time, you will still feel significantly better. The saying is true: practice makes perfect.

Is the R&R Technique just a quick fix, or will the results last?

The majority of my clients say that their most painful burnout symptoms went away and have not returned. Personally, since practicing the technique, my DTEs are gone. Eight years after my recovery from burnout, I haven't looked back. Even when life triggers disturbing emotions, I now have a tool to free them from becoming trapped in my body.

I often compare the R&R Technique to brushing your teeth. I suggest you do it regularly so it becomes an almost unconscious habit. Why? We're human, and life happens; feelings will come up that need to be released.

If I quit doing the R&R Technique, will my disturbing thoughts and emotions come back?

Life will continue to happen. Certain events will occur that will potentially trigger an emotional response. However, most people who practice the R&R Technique consistently report that their emotional responses are shorter in duration and lesser in intensity.

What if what's going on inside of me right now feels too painful to deal with? How do I get beyond that pain to practice the R&R Technique?

Whatever your pain may feel like now, no matter its intensity, don't despair. All the R&R Technique asks you to do is identify the emotion you're feeling and locate it in your body. Unlike talk therapy, it doesn't ask you to go inside your mind to revisit it, to try to understand it, or fix it. It only asks you to feel what's going on in your body and allow that energy to release.

On a personal note, in the depths of my burnout, my feelings of despair didn't just terrify me—I felt suicidal. The reason I believe this technique is so effective is because it puts you in control. Remember, the solution is not a matter of your mind—it's a matter of your body.

Why is it important that I deal with my disturbing thoughts and emotions as they're happening?

This is a question that needs to be answered thoroughly.

- Accessing and releasing your DTEs in the moment stops your brain from "thinking" about them. Once your mind gets involved, it can amplify those feelings, taking away the possibility of releasing them.
- By using the R&R practice regularly, you'll discover that noticing and allowing your disturbing thoughts

and emotions to release will become second nature. It may never become unconscious, but it will prevent the build-up of emotions inside you, putting you at risk of falling back into burnout.

- When you're in burnout, your confidence takes a beating. Practicing the R&R Technique will begin to override the negative monologue in your head that insists there's no hope. It will re-instill hope, belief in yourself, and confidence

I recently had a conversation with Ethan, who's been working with me one-on-one for some time. One day out of the blue, he said, "I can't tell you when it happened exactly, but my burnout is gone." I've heard similar statements from many clients. At some point, they realize that the elephant that's been sitting on their chest, the immense weight of burnout, is simply gone.

I must warn you that when this feeling of relief happens, it can be disconcerting. You may worry that it will come back or wonder if it's just beginner's luck. I promise you that if you practice the R&R technique regularly, the elephant won't return.

The R&R Technique

I want to share the R&R technique now so you can take advantage of it and begin experiencing relief right away.

If you master the Relaxation and Release technique, it will make every other tool and strategy I share easier in the long term.

Please read the instructions carefully because you're about to take a significant step forward in your recovery. Although the directions appear detailed, the practice is remarkably easy to do. Remember, you don't have to believe it will work. You only have to do it.

R&R TECHNIQUE INSTRUCTIONS
NOTICE | INHALE | RELAX | EXHALE | RELEASE

Step 1: *Notice*—Gently notice your thoughts and feelings in this moment. The easiest thoughts and feelings for you to notice are most often the ones that are bothering you. So whenever you're feeling upset, depressed, anxious, stressed, or burnt out, notice your thoughts and feelings. This is important: Notice your thoughts and feelings without trying to suppress, avoid, or fix them. Simply notice them. That's all that you have to do.

Step 2: *Inhale*—Inhale deeply through your nose.

Step 3: *Relax*—Relax your neck, your shoulders, and your whole body to the greatest degree possible.

Step 4: *Exhale*—Exhale through your mouth.

Step 5: *Release*—As you exhale through your mouth, picture your heart opening to release the disturbed energy. Like an uncapped fire hydrant on a hot day in August, shooting water high into the sky, picture cool water flowing out from the center of your chest. This trapped energy has a lot to do with the perception it is protecting you from any potential danger or threats. For now, visualize your heart opening to release it.

The sixth step of the R&R Technique is *"just do it."* You don't have to believe that the technique will work. You don't have to subscribe to any philosophy. All you need to do is practice it consistently. So please—just do it.

Start right now. Do the R&R technique as you continue to read further. Practice it whenever you notice that you are feeling disturbed, upset, or anxious. I guarantee you'll experience positive results.

CHAPTER 5

The Unseen Catches

If you follow the steps I outline in this book, recovering from burnout can be a straightforward process. However, there are a few catches to be aware of so they don't hamper your success.

At this point, you shouldn't be surprised that the three primary catches to my process are internal—because they involve relying on the mind to fix the problem or avoid it altogether.

Catch #1 – "I'm too smart for this to work."

People experiencing burnout tend to be very smart. They often believe that they have a sixth sense, which allows them to predict the future. However, in a burnout mindset driven by fear and despair, the future they dread most often materializes. Like Job says in the Bible, "What I feared has come upon me."

What I've found is that no one is too dumb to find success using my system. However, it is possible to be too smart. Meaning, the only real obstacle in getting the results you desire is if you fail to *follow the process*. In other words, my framework is specifically designed to help very smart, very successful people get out of their own way. I say this with deep affection and empathy because as the first person to use my framework, initially, I believed I was too "smart" for it. My early and somewhat flippant approach was: *I'm in real pain, please don't trivialize what I'm feeling by telling me to do something that sounds so simple.* Needless to say, this attitude got in the way of my recovery.

As a result, I created a system with smart people in mind. That said, early on, this process may feel intellectually unsatisfying. It may feel invalidating. However, what can feel so counterintuitively simple can actually be quite challenging. The R&R technique is a perfect example. How can the process of "*Notice, Inhale, Relax, Exhale, Release*" possibly be all that it takes to free you from the most severe burnout symptoms? It may feel like weak tea at first, but once you start practicing the R&R Technique, you realize it's different from anything you've ever tried before to resolve your burnout.

As I've said, it was the counterintuitive part that first began to make sense to me. If everything I've tried before is failing me, why not try something completely different? But that question can trigger your mind to tell you, *this can't possibly be the answer.* When it does, just recognize that it is your mind telling you this. Although your mind has served as a powerful tool in your life and in your success, it also got you into burnout—the one problem your mind hasn't been able to solve for you. Recovery from burnout is a matter of your body, not your mind.

So, I'm asking you to try something different so you can begin to get out of your own way.

Catch #2 – "I'm too busy to make time for one more thing."

High achievers in burnout are, by definition, *compulsively* busy. I get that, and it's the reason why the Burnout Breakthrough System is composed of powerful exercises that only take five to 10 seconds to complete. Trust me, you have time to do these few simple exercises.

That said, if you want to succeed in your recovery, you must make this process your number one priority. If you're reading this book, I have no doubt that, professionally, you are naturally hardwired to strive for the next level of excellence- making it your top priority. However, what I'm asking you to do might be more challenging—to make *your* mental and physical health the priority. Why is it challenging? For so long, you have been hard-charging. You've taken on more responsibility, and run toward any professional fire necessary to support the people in your life. You have always put the well-being of others ahead of yourself.

Sometimes, for the overachiever, it's hard to let go of these learned habits of doing more and charging harder because we consider them badges of honor. But it is necessary to let go and make your escape from burnout the priority.

I will be honest, your burnout breakthrough won't happen overnight. It will be a process that requires consistency over time and a huge leap of faith on your part. But you can trust my system has worked for my clients, for me, and for the initial group of six people sitting in folded chairs in a circle in my basement. Since then, the circle of people escaping burnout to newfound freedom has grown beyond my wildest imagination.

This process may not work instantly, but it will work quickly, and more importantly, it will deliver long-lasting results. I think about it in terms of the different medications you might have taken. Some are designed to act immediately and bring instant relief. While others are meant to be released gradually into the bloodstream, delivering the same relief but over an extended period of time. The goal of the Burnout Breakthrough System is similar to the latter medication—to bring long-lasting relief to your burnout symptoms.

If you're impatient for a quick solution—first, take a hard, honest look at things you've tried before that might have delivered results but whose benefits didn't last. Sometimes these short-term "fixes" risk triggering an entirely new set of problems.

With the *Burnout Breakthrough System*, make the time. I've designed it specifically for compulsively busy people to be able to implement into their lives.

Catch #3 – "I can't face what I'm feeling—it's too painful, and I'm already in enough pain."

I recognize that the pain of burnout is real and, at times, can feel untouchable. You're like a kid with a scraped knee who hides it from Mom because you fear the sting of the antiseptic you know she's going to use. Let me emphasize that my process is intended to be gentle. In the least painful way possible, the R&R Technique is designed to reveal the specifics of your pain and burnout symptoms that are unique to you. Remember, the technique doesn't ask you to do anything with those feelings or to make them go away—you only need to notice them.

Yes, you will be asked to feel your own pain—more specifically, to notice your burnout symptoms. For years, maybe decades, you've turned to your mind to fix the pain or run from it—to avoid it. To paraphrase Jack Nicholson in *A Few Good Men*, you've convinced yourself that *you can't handle the pain!* And by the time we fall into burnout, we've trained ourselves to believe that leaning into our pain—even a small amount—will bring us to our knees. We're convinced that to pause to even consider the pain we feel, we won't be able to bear it.

think about myself as a young child who was frightened of the monster that I believed lived under my bed. With fear in the driver's seat, I was too terrified to look under my bed. The longer I tried to avoid coming face to face with my imagined monster, the bigger and scarier it became in my mind. Then, one day, I summoned the courage to take a look under my bed; the monster turned out to be nothing more than a balled-up pair of socks and a few dust bunnies. No monster.

It's no different with our disturbed feelings. When we're stuck on fixing and avoiding them, our fears about them grow bigger and scarier, like the perceived monster waiting under my bed. Unintentionally, we train and retrain our minds and our bodies to believe that our disturbing thoughts and emotions are far too scary to deal with. The *Burnout Breakthrough System* is meant to help you "look under your bed" in the safest and least triggering way possible. When you trust in the process and recognize that your pain and fears might only be dust bunnies, the freedom you gain is worth more than any brief moment of discomfort you might experience. It is the freedom you've searched for your entire life.

The R&R Technique is similar to exposure therapy in that it helps you deal with your fears in bite-size pieces. For example, say you're deathly afraid of flying. Using exposure therapy, you may start by watching a brief YouTube video on the mechanics of how a plane flies. When you see that you've survived that, the next step might be driving out to your local airport to watch planes take off and land. Each incremental step builds your courage, so bit by bit, you realize there's nothing to fear. After enough exposure, our fear subsides, and you're ready to board a plane and actually take off.

You already know that the key to freedom from burnout is the R&R Technique. But now I need to share the third R.

The Third "R"

Most likely, this book is not your first attempt to relieve your burnout symptoms. Perhaps, like me, you've tried yoga, meditation, and even biofeedback devices that are supposed to reduce your anxiety, lower your heart rate, and improve your sleep. As mentioned earlier, relaxation by itself is not enough. You can do all the relaxing in the world, but if your disturbing thoughts and emotions remain in place, so will your burnout. It's like planting green grass over a toxic waste site—it may look nice, but the toxic stuff still lies just beneath the surface. That's the genius of the R&R Technique. In addition to doing the first R, *Relaxation*, it must be done in conjunction with the second R, *Release*. When you release those DTEs, when you give them permission to leave, you will feel a dramatic difference in your body—that feeling is the third R, *Relief*.

For a lot of us, "not letting go" is one of our superpowers. We're like a dog with a bone. Over time, we've come to believe our hard-charging nature, our stress, and our anxiety are the uranium rods fueling our overachieving nuclear reactor, powering everything we do. So it sounds counterintuitive when I tell you that to escape burnout, you have to first let go of all of those things. However, a reminder—the R&R Technique is intended to be gentle. It won't ask you to remove all of the uranium rods in your reactor at once. Instead, it asks you to power down each one to zero.

Unlocking the Benefits of the R&R Technique

The R&R Technique is the key that will open the door to the rest of your recovery from burnout. However, the technique alone is not enough. Why? Because the ultimate goal for you and me is permanent recovery—a way of living that will allow us to break through burnout for good and enjoy a life of freedom. The R&R technique on its own will change your point of view, but it's not the whole solution.

Once you learn to practice the R&R Technique to release your DTEs, there's an additional step necessary in your recovery process.

A SIDEBAR: "The Tension Wants to Go"

The tension in your body wants to go. When we experience a sudden shock, we immediately go into "fight-or-flight," and our body dispenses the dosage of adrenaline and cortisol we need to either stand our ground and fight or run like hell. But our bodies aren't designed to stay in fight-or-flight permanently. It isn't physically sustainable. Our sympathetic nervous system can't maintain a perpetual hyper-vigilant state of fight-or-flight. It will eventually fail. That's when we enter burnout.

Picture the release of those DTEs. When they leave your body, they also leave a space in your life, a void that needs to be filled with something different. Since these disturbing thoughts and emotions have acted as your default guidance system until you began your recovery, you need a new GPS. Not the one that sits on your car dashboard—but a new system that will guide you to begin to reclaim the life you gave up to burnout. The new GPS you build will help return you to the positive values that will fuel your burnout-free life. In short, you will construct a new way of thinking—a new way of being- guided by a new GPS.

PART 2

Burnout Breakthrough System

CHAPTER 6
Finding Your New GPS

At the core of the *Burnout Breakthrough System* is your new "Guiding Principles System," or your new GPS. Stephen Hayes, the father of Acceptance and Commitment Therapy (ACT), refers to this repositioning as "getting out of your mind and into your life."[8] It begins with the consistent practice of R&R. As we discussed earlier, the technique alone isn't the entire solution. Yes, it teaches you how to release your DTEs, giving you the freedom to reconsider your life choices moving forward. But once released, the space that is left in your mind and body needs to be filled with something different—something that will sustain freedom from burnout.

In other words, if our negative thoughts and emotions no longer guide our lives, what will we use as our "true north" moving forward? The answer is that instead of letting fear and anxiety, the sustenance of your DTEs, drive your decisions, you substitute the values that are most meaningful to you. For many of us, this return to our values can trigger shame and guilt because we recognize how long we allowed these

---

8 https://scottbarrykaufman.com/podcast/get-mind-live-vital-life-steven-hayes/

destructive thoughts and emotions to override our feelings, our thoughts, and our beliefs.

When you experience the relaxation and release of disturbing thoughts and emotions, you have begun your recovery from the despair of burnout. And somewhere along the way, you discover a very critical truth: *You are NOT your thoughts.* Or, at the very least, you understand that while you can't *eliminate* your thoughts, you can stop letting them bully you into actions that—as Dialectical Behavior Therapy creator Marsha Linehan states, "won't build you a better life."

When you begin to see some daylight between your DTEs and who you really *are*—and, more importantly, the person *you want to become,* you recognize that there's another way of living—a life beyond the negative thoughts and feelings that have kept you caged inside burnout. Constructing a new guidance system that is based on values and principles that are most meaningful to you is the first step to building a better life.

Real recovery from burnout requires not just the absence of burnout symptoms, it requires both discarding our old, defective life compass and embracing an entirely new directional device—one that's based on who you really are and what you really love and value. With this new device at the helm, you can live a life few people dare to hope for.

I will talk in more depth about the Guiding Principles System later in the book. For now, I want to draw an important distinction between the values that lie at the heart of your new GPS—and your goals. Setting and chasing goals is something most overachievers have dedicated their entire lives to. So, I'm not advocating that to recover from burnout, you stop setting or achieving goals. What I am asking you to do is get honest about the goals you've achieved in your lifetime—either individually or collectively. Have those goals led to permanent happiness or, in this case, recovery from burnout? The honest answer is most likely no because it is impossible to attain every goal you set. Failure is inevitable, and so is the shame and frustration that often come with it

What is possible—and, in my experience, more valuable— is finding peace and satisfaction by living according to principles that are truly important to you. In other words, living according to the values that lie at the heart of who you are as a human being. The only way to do this is by creating a new Guiding Principles System.

The future success of your new GPS depends on your acceptance that in order to recover permanently from burnout, you need to replace the broken compass guided by your DTEs. As leadership coach and author Marshall Goldsmith put so eloquently, "What *got* you here won't *get* you there."[9] You need a new guidance system to get you to the freedom that awaits you beyond burnout.

Identifying these core values will not only take you out of burnout, but it will also ensure that you never return. I'm

---

9 What Got You Here Won't Get You There: How successful people become even more successful Paperback – International Edition, June 12, 2008 by Marshall Goldsmith

not referring to moral values—"right or wrong," but rather the things in life that you value and love most—the things that motivate you for all the right reasons. When you shift your energy to these things of value instead of allowing them to be drowned out by your DTEs, you are on the path to live a life of purpose and fulfillment with a new GPS in place.

Holocaust survivor and author Viktor Frankl makes a strong case for this idea in his bestselling book *Man's Search for Meaning*. Frankl attended medical school in Vienna and was a practicing psychiatrist before the Nazis deported him and his family to the Theresienstadt concentration camp in 1942 and then later to Auschwitz, where he lost both of his parents to the gas chambers.

However, in the midst of unspeakable tragedy, Frankl remained a thoughtful observer of his human condition and that of other concentration camp inmates. He noticed the strong correlation between those who survived and their ability to connect to a life purpose, even in the most horrific circumstances. Frankl argues that believing in something greater than themselves was key to their survival. Those without a guiding principle to carry them through found their experience difficult, if not impossible, to survive.

Building Your New Guiding Principles System

When I work with clients to build their new GPS, I start with a values identification exercise. In Chapter 7.2, you will have the chance to complete this exercise on your own.

But first, I want to give a brief overview of how it works and why.

1. From a list of 200 "values" words, clients select the 10 words that mean the most to them.

2. Through a process of elimination, they whittle that list of 10 down to the three or four most meaningful values.

After the elimination process, I encourage clients to "test-drive" their values to make sure their new GPS leads them in the right direction. I would encourage you to go through the same steps, beginning with selecting the 10 words that are most meaningful to you.

Here are a few examples of the value words you may choose. Is *abundance* meaningful in your life? Or is finding *joy*? Or is the pursuit of excellence what fulfills you, or perhaps it's adventure?

Before choosing your value words, I recommend first considering the achievements you've attained in your life that you hold most dear. Then, ask yourself, "Are these the things that life is really about?" Or were many of your achievements fool's gold that led you into burnout? Maybe when you reached for something, it felt meaningful, shiny, and bright—but once you attained it, did it quickly lose its luster?

Until I recognized the difference between fool's gold and real gold—what held meaning in my life and what didn't—I struggled to reconnect with the values that made my life meaningful beyond achievement. To find true meaning—the real gold in my life—I had to surrender my old, defective compass for a new GPS. The same will be true for you. When you find a new guidance system, it will become the lasting solution that turns your life around, making it unimaginably better than even your best day before burnout.

But the step before you do the values exercise to find your new GPS is to take the Beyond Burnout Values Assessment. So, if you haven't taken it yet, I highly recommend you do. As indicated, you can find it in the resource section.

At this moment, the idea of reconnecting to your values may feel overwhelming—and that's completely normal. But again, I'm not asking you to believe this exercise will work. I'm only asking you to do the work. To give this process a try and bring yourself out of burnout for good—using a system that is deceptively simple and effective.

Let me ask you—isn't it time to admit that your solutions to burnout aren't working?

Your struggle can stop right now—you can begin a life beyond your dreams. When you put down the broken compass of DTEs that led you to the exhaustion and defeat of burnout and replace it with a new GPS based on the values most meaningful to you, you will quickly regain your energy, clarity, and confidence. You'll move beyond the false starts of trying to escape burnout and discover a life worth living.

It's your turn to access that life. Just do the work.

CHAPTER 7.0
Extinguishing Burnout

Before we dive into my *Burnout Breakthrough System*, I want to give you a clearer understanding of how the recovery process works.

The three primary symptoms most people experience in burnout are lack of motivation, disconnection, and exhaustion. In previous chapters, we discussed that the first step is to reclaim your energy and physical passion for life by practicing the R&R Technique. My hope is that you've already started using this exercise and are beginning to see results.

Recovering Your Energy and Passion for Life

If we think about recovery in broader terms, elite Olympic athletes take their recovery time as seriously as their training. They understand that recovery allows their muscles to repair and rebuild after exertion, preventing injury or muscle tears. This attitude toward recovery is the complete opposite of the American worker's concept of recovery—working 50 weeks a year and taking only two weeks off to "recover."

However, the science of recovering from stress is more aligned with the elite athlete's approach. For example, Dr. Christina Maslach argues that true recovery happens through regular breaks multiple times a week—not by pushing through long hours and relying on weekends to recharge. Yet, many of us tell ourselves over the weekend, "I'll catch up on my sleep," or "Maybe I'll play a little golf." It's a comforting idea, but as Maslach's work demonstrates, it's not how the human mind and body truly recover.

The key to recovering your energy and passion for life is to notice when you're stressed. When we're deep in burnout, we may recognize our stress but choose to ignore it—pushing through and proudly labeling it as resilience. Highly motivated people often worry that if they notice and acknowledge their feelings, it will lead them down a rabbit hole of self-pity. But noticing your stress *in the moment* is the first step toward recovery. That's why I intentionally designed the R&R Technique to take no more than five seconds to complete. Your challenge is to commit to using it multiple times a week—just as Maslach advocates.

A reminder: Along with noticing, you must be willing to sit with uncomfortable feelings without trying to force them away, as we're often taught to do. This technique is intentionally gentle, asking you to simply coexist with those difficult feelings and then allow them to leave.

Restoring Your Motivation

When we're burned out, there is a direct correlation between our lack of motivation and our lack of confidence.

The path to regain both is to reconnect with your purpose. Finding your purpose means that instead of unconsciously following what your DTEs dictate you do—like the school bully taking your lunch money—you work to identify the guiding principles that ground you in who you really are, according to your new GPS.

This brings us back to the question: What is your true north? What is truly valuable in your life that can help you transcend your DTEs? You don't ignore these feelings. Instead, you'll lean into them, release them, and then recalibrate according to your new GPS to move closer to your true north.

My aha moment came when I realized I had a choice: I could either let these destructive thoughts "bully me," or I could stand up to the bully and turn toward my guiding principles and values, which are connected to my true north. You have the same choice.

As you progress in your recovery from burnout, you'll regain motivation and confidence and start to feel hopeful again. Then, the next question you ask yourself is, what are you going to bet your life on? Are you going to placate and appease your DTEs, leaving them in charge? Or will you focus on the values most meaningful to you and let your new GPS be your guide? For me, the choice was simple.

Later, I will share an exercise that will audit your values, meaning it will assess whether the actions you are taking align with your values and what truly matters to you. As people experiencing burnout, we often find ways to work around our DTEs that are inconsistent with our true values. Once you learn to align your actions with your guiding principles, you take away the power of your negative emotions to manipulate you, setting you on the path to lead a meaningful life free of burnout.

Reclaiming Connection

Feeling disconnected is one of the most debilitating consequences of burnout. You often feel disconnected from your coworkers, friends, and even your spouse and kids. This isolation can burn bridges to the most meaningful relationships in your life. But through my framework, there is hope. The practices and tools you will learn create the possibility of making those key relationships deeper and more meaningful than before burnout.

Often, it's our resentment toward others that lies at the heart of these broken connections, and it's usually because we have been lulled into holding others responsible for our spiral into burnout. When we are able to clearly look at the resentments we've built up, only then do we realize that many were displaced because of our desire to blame our burnout on others. It can become a cycle of self-victimization. It's much easier to blame others than to admit that burnout is an inside job.

When you can admit that you are the problem, the practice of forgiveness can begin—not just to forgive the people who you've directed your resentment toward, but to transform those negative feelings into loving ones—and sincerely wish them well. It's the path toward the reconnection you desire.

Now, it's time to talk about the structure of the *Burnout Breakthrough System*. There are three pillars: Recovery, Transformation, and Preservation. Each pillar will have its own subchapter, complete with practical exercises you can implement in your life immediately. By the time you reach the last page of this book, you'll be several steps closer to freedom from burnout and the fulfilling, purpose-driven life you desire.

One last thing: To make sure you get the most out of my *Burnout Breakthrough System*, head to the resource section at the back of the book, where you can access the links for the exercises in the coming chapters. Download the PDFs so as you're reading, the exercises are right there to complete as we go through the material.

My intention is that by the end of Chapter 7.3, you will have taken steps closer to your recovery from burnout.

CHAPTER 7.1

Burnout Recovery

Recovery

The first pillar of the *Burnout Breakthrough System* is Recovery, which includes three breakthrough concepts. This pillar addresses the primary symptoms most people experience when they begin this work—symptoms outlined in the World Health Organization's definition of burnout, with exhaustion being the most prominent. Use the R&R technique to start regaining your energy—so it's easier to implement the framework effectively.

1. Breaking Through Burnout with Continuous Recovery

To recover from the exhaustion of burnout, we must practice recovery every day. We must get rid of the mentality that you're just one good night's sleep away from recovery—or a long weekend, or a week's vacation, or a 90-day sabbatical—a short period of time where burnout supposedly disappears. This is a gambler's mentality that never pays off because your mind, body, and spirit don't work that way.

What does work is taking many "mini-vacations" throughout the day in addition to practicing recovery multiple times each day. Simply put, when it comes to your physical and psychological stress, you need to recover completely every day—and take steps to do so throughout the day.

This idea is counterintuitive to what many Americans believe—that we can take in all the physical and psychological stress, hold our breath indefinitely, and then take a big sigh of relief when we finally get some time away. That doesn't work. The only way to recover is by noticing when we're stressed in the moment and then releasing that stress.

Noticing

As people experiencing burnout, this is challenging because we've turned not noticing or ignoring our stress into an art form. Whenever we feel physical or mental stress, we slap a Band-Aid over it and keep pushing forward. But not noticing our stress is what disconnects us from what we're truly experiencing in the moment because we've suppressed our feelings for so long.

As you know, the R&R Technique not only requires you to notice—it also involves identifying where you're experiencing stress in your body. Is it a tightness in your stomach? A pain in your shoulder? The easiest and most effective way for people who are burned out to break free from their "numbness" is to pay attention to what's happening in their minds and bodies.

We've established that modern behavioral science says:

- Daily mini vacations are more effective than a weekend in Cabo.

- Releasing your stress *completely* in the moment you experience it is key.

So why is this so difficult? Simple: *We refuse to take the time.* We tell ourselves—we're stressed. We're busy. *We don't have the time.* But it's a critical practice—and it only takes five to 10 seconds.

A Pro Tip to Get This Done:

A Clean Getaway

People who are burned out do everything they can to save time. They tell themselves, "I'll just give myself a few quiet moments at my desk to let this stress go away." Here are three easy techniques to completely disengage from the stress of your work:

- *Get up from your desk and walk around the office.*
- *If you're at home, go outside and walk around the block.*
- *Silence your cell phone—for two minutes.*

Why is "complete" stress release important? The main cause of burnout is twofold: Your stress becomes chronic, and it goes unrelieved over a long period of time. Here's the thing—many people who are burned out spend most of their time trying to control their stress. But the truth is, the more you try to control your stress, the more frequent and intense it becomes.

For context, Dr. Maslach compares burnout and recovery to sprinting. A sprinter runs a 100-meter dash and then takes a break to recover. However, unlike sprinters, people experiencing burnout don't take breaks. They mistake sprinting for a marathon and just keep going—pushing through the 26.2 miles—most often with little success.

Recovery – Action Steps

In addition to the R&R Technique, here are a few important steps you can take that will bring quick results and begin to improve how you feel on a daily basis.

1. **Sleep Hygiene:** Most people understand the importance of a good night's sleep for positive physical and mental health. However, we live in an age when our lives are increasingly saturated with technology, and our attachment to our various devices can run deep—even into the hours when we're supposed to be clocked out. If you never "unplug," you'll never really rest.

My challenge to you, starting tonight, is to develop a shutdown sequence 30 to 60 minutes before bedtime:

- Plug your phone into the charger and leave it there.
- Power down your laptop and tablet.
- Turn off the TV and radio.

Basically say "good night" to any devices that keep your mind from relaxing. If you practice this shutdown sequence nightly, you will train your mind to wind down from the day, which will set you up for a much better night's sleep—a wonderful tool that will enhance your recovery process.

2. **Diet**: Track what you eat and drink during the day by keeping a food journal to identify patterns in how you eat:

Food Journal example:

Day	Breakfast	Lunch	Dinner	Snacks	Notes
Monday	Pop Tart, coffee	2 slices pizza	Big Mac and fries	Chips and salsa	Felt tired, sluggish

When we're in burnout, we tend to load up on our "comfort foods." Judging by the example above, those foods mainly consist of sugar and carbs. They can become like a mood-altering drug that we reach for whenever we're sad or frustrated. Deep in burnout, mood issues are often a result of our addiction to sugar, caffeine, carbohydrates, and alcohol—which may make you feel better in the short term. However, long term, they only contribute to your mood problems. No matter if your "drug" is Starbucks, cookies, or ice cream, your high mood is always followed by a crash. How do we pick ourselves up from that low? You reach for another cookie or another candy bar—and the vicious cycle continues.

The best way to break that cycle is to track what you eat and when you eat. Identify your comfort foods—and replace them with foods that don't contain sugar, are low in carbs, and will sustain you longer. (Hint: add more protein and foods that aren't processed.)

3. **Hydration**: If we go back to the evil trio of sugar, caffeine, and alcohol—in addition to wreaking havoc

on your blood sugar—these three also dehydrate your body. And being dehydrated can play a key role in your burnout exhaustion. The Mayo Clinic suggests the following guidelines for hydration:

Daily fluid intake –

Men	**15.5 cups/day** (124 fl. oz.)
Women	**11.5 cups/day** (92 fl. oz)

In practical terms, a common sports water bottle has a 20-ounce capacity. So for men, that's six bottles per day, for women, around four. I know it sounds like a lot, but the truth is most people—burned out or not—don't hydrate enough. The key is to hydrate throughout the day. If you live in a hot climate or do vigorous exercise, you will probably require more hydration to compensate for the liquid your body loses through perspiration.

Pro tip: Carry a water bottle with you throughout the day. Hydrate when you're driving. When you're sitting at your computer. Sitting on the couch scrolling or watching TV. The more you reach for your water bottle and not a Starbucks coffee, hydrating will become a habit—something you just do.

4. **Getting a Complete Physical:** A recent study by the Cleveland Clinic shows that only three out of five men get an annual physical. According to the same study, more than 40% of men won't go to the doctor unless they believe something is seriously wrong. This behavior is typical of most people who are burned out. If we skin our knee, we rub dirt on it and move

on—not a smart strategy when it comes to your health (as many people discovered during the pandemic). A complete physical can reveal a number of underlying conditions that may be contributing to your burnout:

- Cardiovascular issues (e.g. hypertension)
- Thyroid conditions (e.g. hyperthyroidism)
- Type 2 diabetes

My intention isn't to scare you. It's to encourage you to schedule a complete physical with a qualified physician to assess the state of your health as you begin your recovery—so you know how to take care of yourself through the process.

2. "Breaking Through Disturbing Thoughts and Emotions with Awareness"

At this stage of burnout recovery, there's a critical concept of resistance you most likely will face: *The harder we try to control disturbing thoughts and emotions, the stronger and more frequently we experience them.*

We touched on this before—this step in the process is counterintuitive, because it asks you to let go of the strategies and tactics that worked for you (until they didn't). It's one of the most difficult things for our logical mind to accept.

Fight-or-flight is humankind's fundamental instinct that goes back to our caveman days. The fact that you and I are still around is evidence that our ancestors honed their fight-or-flight instinct to a higher level than those clans who are no longer here. Fight-or-flight works in lots of situations.

Unfortunately, it does not work with our thoughts and emotions. Whatever DTEs we try to fight or flee from come back stronger than before. So, if fight-or-flight is not the answer, what is?

Simply said: *We learn to accept thoughts and feelings as just thoughts and feelings.*

It's a deceptively simple idea. I compare it to the gallbladder, the little pear-shaped organ between your liver and your stomach that contains bile to help you digest fat. Every day your gallbladder just does what it does without any of our attention or awareness.

Your brain is also an organ that, day in and day out, monitors many body functions that we're not conscious of. But our brain also happens to be where our thoughts and feelings originate. We tend to be very aware of them and take them very seriously—unlike the function of our gallbladder—where we have no awareness and thus no opinions.

When it comes to our thoughts and feelings, we definitely have opinions. Remember when I mentioned Michael Singer's Acceptance and Commitment Therapy? In his acronym (ACT), the "A" stands for "acceptance"—accepting your thoughts and feelings as merely thoughts and feelings. Meaning it isn't necessary for you to take your thoughts and feelings any more seriously than you take your gallbladder when it produces bile.

Your brain produces thoughts and feelings to keep you alive—whereas your gallbladder produces bile to keep you alive *without any thoughts or feelings attached.* But we tend to take thoughts and feelings very personally—so personally that we've become convinced that we can't be successful unless we control them.

I want to share a questionnaire I give to my clients to help them recognize their level of connection to their thoughts, feelings, and beliefs—and determine whether controlling them plays a defining role in their success and happiness.

Take a moment to go through the questionnaire. (There are only eight questions—so you have time.)

Control of Thoughts and Feelings Questionnaire

This assessment is based on the evidence that shows:

a. *The brain creates thoughts and emotions automatically, much like our pancreas produces insulin;*

b. *We cannot control which thoughts and emotions come up, nor do we need to for happiness and success.*

c. *Trying to control or avoid thoughts and emotions often makes them more frequent.*

d. *We are only responsible for the actions which we can control.*

Please select the statement that best reflects how you feel right now. There are no "right" or "wrong" answers. The answer you choose doesn't have to be true 100% of the time. Just choose the response that's mostly true for you.

1. **Control of Feelings**
   - ☐ A. I must control my feelings to be successful.
   - ☐ B. It's unnecessary to control my feelings for success.
2. **Nature of Anxiety**
   - ☐ A. Anxiety is bad.
   - ☐ B. Anxiety is just an uncomfortable feeling.
3. **Impact of Negative Thoughts**
   - ☐ A. Negative thoughts can harm me if not controlled.
   - ☐ B. Negative thoughts don't harm me, even if they feel unpleasant.
4. **Fear of Feelings**
   - ☐ A. I'm afraid of my strong feelings.
   - ☐ B. I'm not afraid of any feelings, no matter how strong.
5. **Doubts and Important Actions**
   - ☐ A. I need to eliminate doubts to do something important.
   - ☐ B. I can act on important tasks even with doubts present.
6. **Dealing with Negative Thoughts**
   - ☐ A. It's important to reduce negative thoughts quickly.
   - ☐ B. Allowing negative thoughts to exist naturally helps.
7. **Managing Negative Emotions**
   - ☐ A. Analyzing negative emotions is the best way to manage them.

☐ B. Acknowledging negative emotions without judgment is more effective.

8. **Perception of Negative Emotions**

☐ A. Negative feelings indicate psychological issues.

☐ B. Negative feelings are a normal part of being human.

When you've answered all eight questions, total your "A" responses.

Rating Scale:

Zero to one "A's": You understand that you can't control thoughts and don't need to in order to be successful and happy in your life.

Two to three "A's": You feel you have some control over your thoughts and feelings, and you believe that you need to manage them.

Four to eight "A's": You have an unrealistic view of your control over thoughts. The good news is that you can learn to release this habit to live a happier life. Through the steps in my framework, you will learn how to stop trying to control them and simply notice them and then completely release them.

This way, instead of trying to exert control over them, you will learn to coexist with them. You are not your thoughts and emotions.

3. "Breaking Through Depression and Anxiety with Presence and Detachment"

An important fact to understand: *Burned-out people tend to live either in the past or in the future.*

As people experiencing burnout, we tend to obsess about the future and its potential catastrophes waiting for us. We also focus on our past and can stay stuck there. For now, I want to concentrate primarily on our future thoughts, using the language of Post-Traumatic Stress Disorder (PTSD)— what we call "hypervigilance."

We touched on this idea earlier. Hypervigilance is a heightened state of awareness where we're constantly scanning our present situation while anticipating potential dangers down the road. It's often falsely based on the belief that we can and must control everything that happens— when the reality is, that you can't control something that can't be controlled. In other words, it isn't possible to anticipate every single thing that might happen to us on a global scale.

Here's the truth: *The only thing that is really real is this moment.*

The moment right now, as you read the words on this page, is the only thing that is actually real—not the future that you anticipate, obsess about, plan for, and worry about. In the words of a dear friend, "*We have to be where our hands are.*" Our hands, not our minds, can only be in the present moment.

The more you tune into your experience in the present moment, the more peace and freedom you'll have to live the way you want to live. The present is the only place you can truly be happy. You can't find happiness if you're obsessed with the future because the future hasn't happened yet—therefore, it isn't real.

I remember a time when my colleague kindly listened to a litany of my worries. When I finished, he said, "Ninety percent of what you worry about will never come to fruition—because everything you just listed isn't real." His statement knocked me back on my heels because, in my mind, I had made all those worries feel far more real than the present moment.

As I processed the truth in his words, I realized that the only time I could be happy was right now. The only time I can ever truly live is now. Now is where we find the peace and freedom to live the way we want to live—free from the stress of fears and worries that aren't real.

Living in the future is a lot like dreaming. When you have a nightmare, you often wake up breathing heavily, your heart pounding. But once you're fully awake, you can see that as scary as the dream was when you were in it, the dream wasn't real. Typically, your fear and anxiety dissipate. It's similar to all of your bad dreams about the future, in other words, your worries—when you're in the present moment, your anxiety and worry disappear. *Be where you are.*

How do you focus your attention on the present when those disturbing thoughts and emotions are trying to drag you into a dark corner? One way that may sound overly simple is to get in touch with your five senses.

THE "5 SENSES" EXERCISE

You can do this exercise anywhere and at any time to reduce your anxiety and help you feel better. It uses your five senses to ground you in the present. Every time you catch yourself obsessing over the future, this exercise can return your mind to where you are.

STEP 1: "See" – Open your eyes and look at what's around you right now in your current environment. Now, name five things that you see. Observe them in detail. Describe to yourself their size, color, texture, and anything else you may see.

EX: I see a large chair covered in dark blue tweed fabric and a dining room table stacked with manila file folders.

STEP 2: "Touch" – Reach out and touch four things around you. Describe the feel of each one—rough, smooth, cool to the touch, or warm. Are they hard or squeezably soft?

EX: "The seat of the chair I'm sitting in is hard and cool to the touch."

STEP 3: "Hear" – Quiet your mind and focus on the sounds around you. Then, identify three. Are they loud or soft? Is the pitch high or low? Are they coming from close by—the room or place you're in—or from farther away?

EX: "I hear the soft hum of the air conditioning fan and the low sound of a TV somewhere else in the house."

STEP 4: "Smell" – Breathe in deeply through your nose. Name two things that you smell right now. Describe them. Are they faint or strong? Sweet—or sour?

EX: "I smell the strong black coffee on the desk in front of me and the smell of pizza coming from the break room."

STEP 5: "Taste" – Focus on your sense of taste. Is there anything you can taste in the present moment?

EX: "I can still taste the ham sandwich I ate an hour ago—sweet, salty, and full of smoky flavors."

This exercise may sound simple—but remember, it's your mind trying to convince you that the solution to your distress must be complicated. I promise that a huge part of the solution can be as simple as grounding yourself in the present and allowing yourself to experience your five senses in the present moment. It's hard to worry about the past or the future if your focus is on the "right now." You can either be "there" or "here." You can't be in both places at once.

By combining the practice of the R&R Technique and the 5 Senses exercise, you can easily and quickly bring yourself back to the present, where you are able to recognize that future dangers are an illusion, so you can relax and feel safe in the present moment.

CHAPTER 7.2

Breakthrough Transformation

The second pillar in the *Burnout Breakthrough* recovery system is called *Transformation* because these steps and practices will lead you through three important and life-changing breakthroughs:

- Breaking through negativity by harnessing values

- Breaking through to purpose by aligning values with actions

- Breaking through to motivation with values-based goals.

1. Breaking Through Negativity by Harnessing Values

The first transformation is based on the idea that, at the end of the day, your thoughts are nothing more than words. If they're helpful words, you should pay attention to them. However, if they're not helpful, then why bother? This raises the question: What makes a thought helpful?

In our burnout world, a thought is helpful only if it enhances your life. Marsha Linehan, the brilliant psychologist, professor emeritus at the University of Washington, and creator of Dialectical Behavior Therapy introduced me to this concept. She offers a simple but powerful "acid test" to determine whether a thought is worth paying attention to: Will these thoughts I'm thinking help me build a better life?

You might be thinking that is all well and good, but *what do I do with my negative thoughts—the ones that keep hijacking my mind and tearing me down?* It's a good question because negative thinking can become deeply habitual with a risk of becoming almost hypnotic—part of the prison walls that keep you in burnout. The answer is simple: *We break through our unhelpful thoughts by harnessing our values.*

The idea of harnessing your values takes us back to the new GPS you're creating (Guiding Principles System), which, at its core, is about finding your true north according to your values. Imagine burnout as being lost in the deepest, darkest forest. It's pitch black, and spooky noises fill the air. Without a GPS to guide you, you risk running in circles—desperate to escape but only ending up where you've already been. This keeps you trapped in that scary place, no closer to the wonderful reality that awaits you beyond burnout.

As you build your new GPS and reconnect with your values, they will prompt you to answer fundamental questions like, *Does this help me take effective action to improve my life?* Only your values will help you gain clarity about what you truly want in life, what you love, and what you hold most dear. When you align your actions and thoughts with your values, you take the disturbing thoughts and emotions out of the driver's seat—thoughts that, for so long, offered you only two options to get free from burnout: fix it or avoid it. We both know how that worked—not well. When your values become your true north in your new GPS—that's when you can attain freedom from burnout.

Let's return to that fundamental question and explore it more deeply. Does this thought help me take effective action to improve my life? Two crucial words stand out in that question—**action** and **improve**. Remember Stephen Hayes, the creator of Acceptance and Commitment Training (ACT)? He put it best: we need to get out of our minds and into our lives—specifically, into building the best possible life for ourselves. How? By identifying and focusing on your values:

- What do I truly love and care about in my life?
- What do I want my life to be about?
- What actions could I take right now to align with what I really care about?

Emerging from burnout requires unlearning old, destructive habits—especially the belief that the only way to overcome burnout is to work harder, push through, and worry more. That's just your DTEs bullying you into staying trapped in burnout exhaustion. Instead, I want you to flip that bad habit on its head and ask yourself: What will build me the beautiful life that I truly want?

I also urge you to take it one step further with a devil's advocate question: What do I gain by buying into this crummy thought?

For example, imagine a persistent negative thought like: *I never do anything right—I always mess up.* Instead of letting it take hold, start from your true north—your values—and ask: What's the payoff for engaging with this thought? Then, go even deeper: If I follow this direction on my emotional compass, where will it lead me?

I can tell you exactly where: straight into the cul-de-sac of despondency and despair. Sound familiar?

These questions help you stay aligned with your values. Here's another powerful one: Who would I be without this negative thought? Each of these questions acts as a guidepost, leading you out of the dark forest of burnout by shifting your actions to align with what truly matters to you.

Because you and I both know—we've let these negative thoughts and emotions run our lives for too long. It's high time we question their validity.

Broken down for you, here's a list of questions to ask:

- Does this thought help me be the person I want to be?
- Does it help me build the kind of relationship I want?
- Does this thought help me connect with what I truly value?

I mentioned this earlier, but here, I want to draw a clear distinction between values and morals. Morality—having morals—means you generally understand right from wrong. **Values**, on the other hand, are the guiding principles that help you create a rich and meaningful life.

When your values become your true north—replacing your DTEs and negative thoughts—you can move toward freedom from burnout. At times, this process may feel scary or uncomfortable. But here's the key difference: when you're guided by your values, you recognize that any DTEs you may experience are temporary, not permanent.

More importantly, as long as you continue taking action to improve your life, you will stay on course—on track and on target—to reach your destination. The more you tune into your direct experience, the more freedom you will have to live the life you truly want.

Values provide a way to stop wasting your precious time trying to fix or avoid your thoughts and emotions. Instead, they point you toward a life you've only dreamed about. And I can tell you this: values work is deeply personal. Without exception, every person I've worked with has experienced a near-immediate return of a positive attitude and sense of purpose the moment they begin moving toward what truly matters to them.

Remember the values identification exercise I discussed earlier? Now it's your turn to complete it. If you haven't already, please print out the PDF located in the resource section.

Values Exercise Part 1

Here's the process:

1. **Pick 10 – Choose the 10 Values from the List Below That Mean the Most to You.** This is just a snapshot

of the full list of values you will find in the resources
section. This shorter list will give you a good start:

Abundance	Comfort	Expert	Foster
Capable	Excellence	Laugh	Magnificence
Enlighten	Integrity	Respond To	Romance
Inspire	Reign	Catalyze	Discover
Radiance	The Unknown	Articulate	Assist
Synthesize	Alert	Conceive	Contentment
Accomplish	Community	Explain	Freedom
Cause	Exhilaration	Learn	Mastery
Enroll	Invent	Responsible	Rule
Instruct	Relate to God	Contributor	To Experience
Realize	Thoughtful	Artistic	Attain
Taste	Alter	Congruent	Control
Acquire	Compassionate	Facilitate	Fun
Coach	Experiment	Love	Minister
Entertain	Joy	Risk	Satisfied
Integrate	Religious	Creator	To Feel
Refine	Thrill	Assemble	Attentive
Tenderness	Arouse	Connection	Courage
Adventure	Complete	Family	Gamble

2. **Review & Condense** – Review your list of 10 and
   cross off three that compared to all of the rest, feel less
   important to you.

3. **Your Top Four** – Now, distill your list again. Take
   another look and eliminate three more values, which
   should leave you with four values remaining.

The values list is intentionally extensive—so you have
plenty of choices—but I encourage you to include any
additional values you don't see listed that are important
to you. Remember, your choice of values is extremely
personal. I'm empowering you to choose the values that
really mean something to *you*—not necessarily the values
of your spouse, your college roommate, your colleague, or
anybody else. These personal values are essential in creating
your **new GPS**—your internal guide for living with purpose.
Your list of values will serve as an affirmation of how you

want to live, aligning your actions with what you love and what brings the greatest meaning to your life.

A fair warning: this exercise gets more challenging the deeper you go. Picking your initial 10 values may feel fairly easy. However, when you're asked to get your list of 10 down to four, it can get difficult. Bear with me. The reason I'm pushing you to make choices is that we're chipping away at the coal mine of murky negative thoughts to uncover the diamond—your new north star. This true north will cut through the gloom of burnout and light the way toward a life of clarity, purpose, and renewal.

Once you have your final four, I suggest living with your values list for a week—the test drive I spoke of earlier. My experience is that people will vacillate a bit. Giving it a few days allows you to see how those core values work as your new compass—you may decide to make some tweaks. That's completely fine—and normal. When you're feeling good about your top four values, finish with this step:

4. **Rank Your Top Four Values from 1 Through 4.** Your most important value should be first, then the second most important next, and so on. These four choices in that order will become the center of your new GPS.

Values Exercise Part 2

The second part of the Values exercise involves some writing:

1. For Each of Your Final Four Values, Write a Brief Paragraph (Around 50 Words).

As you write, take time to reflect on these four questions:

- Why did I choose this value?
- Why is this value important to me?
- What would it mean to live according to this value?
- How would living this value affect my actions?

Read through each paragraph about your top four values. Do you see more clearly now the wrong direction your old guidance system was leading you? Admittedly, shifting your focus toward what you truly value—rather than defaulting to negative thoughts and emotions—is a huge change. It can feel like tough love to put all the bullshit aside and ask yourself, *"How's all that been working for me?"*

I'd venture to guess that since you bought this book and are still reading it, your old GPS hasn't been working. And as overwhelming or uncomfortable as this shift may feel, isn't where you are right now—fearful, exhausted, joyless— reason enough to try something different?

Even if it feels counterintuitive, remind yourself what worked in the past—pushing harder, charging forward— isn't working now. So why not try something new? What do you have to lose?

2. Breaking Through to Purpose by Aligning Values with Actions

This second Transformation Breakthrough is about

reclaiming your true purpose. It begins with aligning the values you just identified with your **actions**—this is where the rubber meets the road.

Once you've pinpointed your top four values, a big shift is about to take place. But I'm not just asking you to face in a general northerly direction. I'm asking you to face your true north with precision and to aim directly for that exact point. This is where you need to commit—to using your new compass to guide your actions as you move forward.

It's not enough to simply identify your values. If you want to step into the life that's waiting for you beyond burnout, you must hold yourself accountable for aligning your behavior with the values that matter most to you. (Don't worry—I'm going to help you with all of this.)

The real test of whether your values are authentic to you is simple: Do they change your behavior? Because without a shift in action, nothing will change. Breaking through burnout isn't about having high aspirations alone—it's about aligning what you say you believe in (your values) with the actions you take moving forward.

Aligning Your Values to Actions Exercise

Grab your four values and the paragraphs you wrote about them because we're going a layer deeper with an exercise that will help you understand what it means to align your actions with your values.

Aligning Exercise Part 1

1. **Values Categories** – On a sheet of paper, write down the following nine categories:

> A. Significant other
>
> B. Family
>
> C. Friends
>
> D. Spirituality
>
> E. Personal development
>
> F. Fun
>
> G. Career
>
> H. Money
>
> I. Legacy

2. **For Each of These Nine Categories, Write Down the Following:**

> 1. **Write Three Values for Each Category.** (Feel free to refer back to the values list for ideas.) Identify them in these terms:
>
>   - How you want to behave (*Example: How do I want to behave with my spouse?*)
>
>   - What impact do you want to have (*Example: What impact do I want to have on my friends?*)
>
>   - What memories do you want to leave behind (*Example: What do I want my legacy to be for my family?*)

Of these, pay special attention to the first one—how you want to behave—because it's all about action. When you begin to align your actions with your key values, an entirely new possibility for living will open up—one that can surpass even your best days before burnout.

At this stage, you need to take it to a granular level—getting specific about how your values will shape your behavior toward your significant other, family, friends, and beyond. For example, I've worked with several business leaders who tell me, *"I want to spend more time with my kids."*

Okay, but now get specific. *How much time? How many hours per week do you want to spend with each child? What will you be doing together?* And more importantly, *how much time do they need from you so that your presence has a positive impact on their lives?*

When we examine how we spend our time, one truth becomes immediately clear: everybody wants it all.

This is the central struggle for overachieving people experiencing burnout—they want success in business. They want thriving professional relationships. They want quality time with their peer group, their friends, their children, and their spouse or significant other.

But here's the reality: "having it all" isn't as simple as it sounds. To explain why, let me introduce you to a metaphor…

Q: *How do you get three rocks, a handful of pebbles, and several scoops of sand to fit into a glass vase?*

A: *If you put the sand in first, followed by the pebbles, you'll never get the rocks in.*

Start with the rocks, then put the pebbles in, and put the sand in last.

Let's go through what this means for our purpose. Imagine you have a large, empty glass jar sitting in front of you. Next to it, you have a collection of rocks, pebbles, sand, and water. Each of these represents different aspects of your life—your biggest priorities, everyday obligations, and the smaller distractions that can fill up your time.

The rocks are the most important things—your core values, your family, your health, your most meaningful relationships, and your true purpose. The pebbles, then, are your secondary priorities, like career achievements, friendships, and hobbies. The sand and water symbolize the small stuff—the daily tasks, emails, social media, and other distractions that consume time but don't necessarily add deep value to your life.

Now, if you pour the sand and water into the jar first, filling it with minor tasks and distractions, there's no room left for the rocks—the things that matter and that you value most. But if you place the rocks in first, then add the pebbles, and finally pour in the sand and water, everything fits.

This is where many overachieving, burned out individuals get it wrong—they try to fit in everything without prioritizing the most meaningful parts of their lives. They start with the small stuff, leaving little room for what matters most.

The key to breaking free from burnout is making sure your rocks go in first. You must intentionally structure your life so that your values dictate your time—not the other way around.

So ask yourself: Are you filling your jar with what you value most first? Or are you letting sand and water take up all the space?

When it comes to kids, their needs have to come first. Here's an example. I have a client with three boys and a girl. His oldest son—his pride and joy—plays football, and he's heavily involved in supporting him. But his younger daughter isn't into sports.

When I asked him, "What does your daughter like to do?" he froze. I clarified, "What does she want your relationship to look like? Have you talked to her about what she enjoys doing with you? Do you know what her interests are?"

He hesitated before answering, "Well, I shoot baskets with her."

So I asked, "Is that what she wants?"

He admitted he wasn't sure. All he knew was that shooting baskets was what he liked to do—not necessarily what she wanted to do.

That was the breakthrough moment. I emphasized that to

truly connect with his daughter, he needed to discover her interests, understand her love language, and recognize what would make her feel valued. In other words, what would fill her bucket in their time together?

Now, turn this question toward your own kids:

Could you answer the same questions I asked my client?

- Do you know what each of your children is truly interested in?
- Have you asked them what they enjoy doing with you?
- What would fill each of their buckets in the time spent together?

Because when it comes to building meaningful relationships with your kids, it's not about what you want to do—it's about what they need from you.

If you want a successful relationship with your child, your spouse, or any of the significant people in your life—and if relationships are one of your highest values—then you have to shift your perspective. Ask yourself: What do they want from this relationship—not what you assume they want, but what they actually need from you? Then, you have to carve out the time to give that to them—intentionally, consistently, and with presence.

The Hard Truth: You Can't Have It All

No one can. Hard choices have to be made because there are only so many hours in a day. As people experiencing burnout, we rationalize the choices we make. We tell ourselves stories to justify cur behavior. We believe our families will appreciate the egregious hours we put in at the office—that all the stress, the late nights, and the sacrifices are for them.

I did this, too. My story? A complete lie, by the way. *I told myself I had to work all those extra hours, or my* wife *and kids would starve.* That was my burnout brain talking. In my mind, my insane hours were saving them from starvation and homelessness—even though my wife told me repeatedly that she didn't give a damn how much money we had.

At one point, she hit me with the harsh truth: *"This is on you. This is your choice."* And she was right. But for us high-achieving, burned out individuals, we don't want to see it that way. Through our egotism and selfishness, we convince ourselves that we're the family hero—the provider, the savior.

But let's call it what it is: bullshit. And deep down, we know it. That's why people who are burned out feel so much guilt and shame. Because beneath all the justifications and rationalizations, we know the real story:

We aren't sacrificing for our families. We're rationalizing our own ambition.

In his seminal book *Walden,* Henry David Thoreau wrote, "The mass of men lead lives of quiet desperation." I would offer that the reason is because we're living contrary to our values. You can't cheat values. We all have them, whether we write them down or not. We also know whether we are living according to them—or not. Look at your top four values from the Alignment Exercise and in which category they fall—family, friends, personal development, etc. Then, ask yourself two questions:

A. Am I actually living according to that value right now? (Is your behavior consistent with that value?)

B. Which value or values am I neglecting or contradicting?

Remember, no one can have it all. If you're neglecting your value of family, for example, that energy is being redirected somewhere else—whether it's work, obligations, or distractions. And while there are seasons in life where certain things must take priority, the key is to check in with yourself regularly and ask:

- What's truly driving me day to day?
- Am I being led by my disturbing thoughts and emotions—mainly ego and fear?
- Or am I being guided by actions that align with the kind of person I really want to be?
- Am I honoring my values by fulfilling the commitments I've made?

These are tough questions—but they're the ones that matter. Because if you can answer them with a resounding yes, then your freedom from burnout and a life driven by purpose is not just possible—it's inevitable.

3. Breaking Through to Motivation with Goals

The third and final transformation breakthrough deals with your goals and the specific outcomes you want. Before we begin, let's talk again about the difference between goals and values. Russ Harris clarifies their distinction in his book, *The Happiness Trap* (highly recommended reading):

> "If you want a better job, that's a goal. Once you've gotten it, the goal is achieved. But if you want to apply yourself fully at work, to be attentive to details, supportive to your colleagues, friendly to customers, and engaged in what you're doing, those are values."
> - Russ Harris, *The Happiness Trap*

To paraphrase, goals are the "what," and values are "how do we want to be?" The reason that goals are so important is that they help turn our values into action. That's why, in the previous section, we talked about how much time you spend in the significant areas of your life and the impact you want to have. See, taking action is not about the past. It's not about the future. It's about dealing with reality *right now* and being present for your life as it unfolds. Consider this thought:

The missing ingredient in most miracles is
the sweaty proof that you are serious.

Most people who are burned out are really good at taking action—with the caveat that most of those actions are directed primarily at fixing or avoiding. The problem is not inaction. The problem comes when your actions, goals, and values aren't aligned. When you have this alignment, you will break through procrastination (which leaves us feeling exhausted, aimless, and hopelessly stuck) to *motivation*. Isn't this what we all dream of?

Goals Lead to Action

When you're recovering from burnout, action is the magic word. Specifically, values-based action is the fastest, most effective way to break through burnout and step into a deeply fulfilling life.

That's why I'm such a strong advocate for Acceptance and Commitment Therapy (ACT)—because it's ALL about action. ACT teaches that the only way to fully engage with life is to take action now—not when conditions are perfect, not when you feel ready, but right now—in service of your values.

Burnout isn't something you think your way out of. You act your way out of it—one step, one decision, one values-aligned choice at a time.

By the time people reach burnout, they've often lost their motivation—and that can be terrifying for them. If that sounds familiar, the shift you may need to make—especially if you're a goal-oriented person—is to realign your goals so they are guided by your values rather than driven by ego, fear, or your old DTEs. Your new values-based goals will replace the old ones that were driven by the need to prove yourself, seek approval, or placate the fears created by your disturbing thoughts and emotions.

Values-based goals serve a **different** purpose:

1. **Values-based goals** are *in service of the person we truly want to be.*
2. **Values-based goals** *have the impact we want them to have.*
3. **Values-based goals** serve the people we care about.

When you shift to values-based goals, you open the door to using your ego in a way that is both healthy and productive. Instead of battling your thoughts and emotions every day—trying to force them away and disappear—you start focusing on something much more meaningful: acting in alignment with your values.

What hasn't worked for you in the past (and it certainly didn't work for me) is waking up every day with the sole goal of making your troubled thoughts and emotions go away. That's a battle you'll never win. Interestingly, many of the values-based goals you set as you come out of burnout may look similar to the ones you had before. But the difference—and it's a big one—is that your motivation will be entirely different.

Reigniting motivation is critical because burnout makes you feel like you've tried and failed at everything to get yourself moving again. And when you can no longer motivate yourself, you feel completely lost—stuck in the cul-de-sac of despair.

The way out? Stop chasing motivation. Start chasing what truly matters to you.

Values-Based Goal-Setting Exercise

This is one of the most powerful exercises in the Beyond Burnout Framework. There are five steps to this exercise to give you some practice in setting values-based goals where your daily motivation is no longer your DTEs but instead fueled by the values in your life.

STEP 1 – **Review: Review the Nine Value Categories from the Aligning Exercise:**

- Significant Other
- Spirituality
- Career
- Family
- Personal Development
- Money
- Friends
- Fun
- Legacy

STEP 2 – **Pick Three:** From those nine categories, choose three that are the most important to you right now. Example: Family/Spirituality/Legacy

(HINT: For most people, all nine categories will have some importance in their lives. But for the purpose of this exercise, choose the three that are your hot buttons today. Remember, you can't do this wrong.)

STEP 3 – **Values-Based Goal-Setting, Short, Medium, and Long:** For each value that you chose, do the following:

a. Set a **short-term goal** that you can do right **now**.

b. Set a **mid-term goal** that you can achieve **in 30 days**.

c. Set a **long-term goal** you can achieve **in 60 days**.

(HINT: A little hesitation is normal. People coming from burnout don't jump at making new goals because many of their old ones have crashed and burned. They don't want more disappointments. But do this exercise with faith and trust that in the process, you'll find the motivation to achieve these short, medium, and long-term goals. Why? They're no longer based on fear but instead on what is important to you.)

STEP 4 – Goals Into Action: For Each of Your Goals from Step 3, Create Three Action Steps as Follows:

a. One **short-term action step** you can complete **now**.

b. One **mid-term action step** you can complete in **30 days**.

c. One **long-term action step** you can complete in **60 days**.

(HINT: There's power in action, and frankly, this is where most of us fall short. We have these great goals, but without taking the appropriate action steps, we get nowhere. Or we're not realistic about the time necessary to complete each step. Big goals are achievable if you have a strategy about how you're going to achieve them by choosing action steps in the short, medium, and long term.)

STEP 5 – **Share Your Goals:** Once you've completed the exercise, email your goals to me at **scott@doubledareyou. us**. Don't worry—I'm not grading your assignment. Instead, you'll receive an email back with a PDF file containing your Values-Based Goals and Action Steps in a concise chart. This chart is designed for you to print out and post somewhere visible—a daily reminder of what you're aiming for and the actions that will keep you aligned with your values.

STEP 6 – **Share with a Group:** We'll dive deeper into the importance of community and accountability in Chapter 8, but for now, start seeking out like-minded people—those who truly understand what you're going through and are also taking steps to change their circumstances for the same reasons you are. A supportive community is the key to breaking free from the isolation cell of burnout. It reconnects you with people who can encourage you, challenge you, and hold you accountable—ensuring that you stay on track and actually succeed in making lasting changes.

Burnout thrives in isolation. Recovery happens in connection.

CHAPTER 7.3

Breaking Through "Overwhelmed" with "Goal-Shedding"

"We have met the enemy and he is us."

~*Walt Kelly*[10]

Because you've made it this far, I want to address a fear you may be experiencing right now—one that I know personally: *"What if this recovery doesn't last?"*

It's a legitimate fear. I felt it, too. I had tried so many things that worked for a while, only to find myself back in burnout again. The cycle felt endless. But I want to reassure you— you can lock in your recovery. That's exactly why the third section of this framework exists. It's specifically designed to ensure that you never slip back into a state of exhaustion and despair. And here's the most important part: This system has been proven. Hundreds of people have followed these steps, and not one person who has completed them has ever relapsed.

---

10   https://www.apa.org/monitor/jun03/sd

You're about to learn exactly how to make your recovery permanent—so you never have to go through burnout again.

As I mentioned earlier, burnout is a deeply ingrained habit that is reinforced by our brain chemistry. So, it's no surprise that if you don't take intentional steps to prevent it, burnout behaviors can resurface.

The good news? Relapsing is 100% preventable—as long as you take advantage of the proven techniques in this section. In fact, as we'll explore in the final section, "Beyond Burnout," relapse isn't just preventable—our clients have reported experiencing a level of peace and fulfillment they never thought possible. I'm grateful to say that was my experience, too.

At first, I would have given my right arm just for a moment of relief from the exhaustion. But what I discovered was far greater than just relief—I felt better than I've ever felt in my life. This is the real opportunity to break through burnout— not just escaping despair and exhaustion for good but stepping into a new level of positivity, achievement, and fulfillment—one that's sustainable, deeply rewarding, and life-changing.

It's a good-news-bad-news story: we cause our own burnout—it's an inside job. But let's focus on the good news. If we are the cause of our burnout, that means we also hold the power to cure it. If recovery depended on waiting for other people to change, we'd be stuck in a never-ending cycle of frustration and disappointment.

But for you, the wait is over. That said, there are habits you need to break—and that's exactly what this section is about. Before we dive into the core of this third pillar of my framework—goal-shedding versus goal-setting—I want you to understand:

- Why our old habits are so hard to break.
- Why this new technique is essential for maintaining your recovery from burnout.

I've touched on some of this before, but now, we're going to go deeper. Through my work with burned-out executives and leaders, I've discovered that they share five common characteristics.

1. *We are very achievement-oriented.* I mentioned this earlier, but it's worth saying again. The trouble with achievement is that, by definition, it is short-lived. There is a beginning, a middle, and an end to every achievement. We tend to be our own harshest critics. As soon as the aura of our achievement fades, the question, "But what have you done lately?" starts nagging at us.

In this sense, achievement functions like an addictive substance—a self-administered injection of brain chemicals that keep us chasing the next high. We become hooked on our own neurochemistry—dopamine, norepinephrine, cortisol, adrenaline—each one fueling our drive for success, validation, and accomplishment. But there's a catch:

Every achievement-induced high has a beginning, middle, and end. No matter how big the win, the rush fades—

and when it does, we instinctively start chasing the next achievement to reclaim that feeling. This cycle is what drives burnout. The relentless pursuit of more exhausts your brain, body, and soul. You've quite literally burned out your brain's ability to keep up—leaving you running on empty, physically, mentally, and emotionally drained.

2. *We are perfectionists.* Like so many aspects of burnout, being a perfectionist used to serve us well. We were rewarded, particularly early in our careers, for our pursuit of perfection in everything we did. Many of us have built a reputation for delivering bulletproof work—for being letter-perfect in everything we do.

The problem? Perfection is impossible. Even for the most meticulous, high-achieving individuals, true, sustained perfection simply doesn't exist. Yes, the pursuit of perfection often leads to high-quality work, but it also traps us in a vicious cycle—one that's impossible to close. The standard we set for ourselves keeps moving further out of reach, and no matter how hard we try, it's never quite enough.

You've likely seen it in your own experience:

- Perfectionism leads to dissatisfaction.
- Dissatisfaction leads to exhaustion.
- Exhaustion fuels more perfectionism.

And so the cycle continues—until burnout brings everything to a screeching halt.

3. *We don't say "no."* This is another way of saying that we

have no boundaries. Early in our careers, not saying "no" paid off. We developed a reputation for being the ones trusted with the most critical tasks because we always delivered, no matter what it cost us. Early in our careers, this yielded rewards, but over time, that fruit turned into a poison apple—especially as our responsibilities grew and our lives—both at work and home—became more complex.

Having no boundaries once had a great payoff. We become superstitious about what has worked for us in the past, asking ourselves, *"Why should I set boundaries now?"* After all, saying "yes" has always worked before. We fear that setting boundaries now might damage our reputation or make us lose our grip on the ladder of success.

My own addiction to having no boundaries made me genuinely afraid that if I delegated work or had the temerity to say "no," it might lead to failure—making it impossible to provide for my family. That disturbing thought and emotion soon became a constant mantra in my mind. And in that echo chamber, I never stopped to consider that the mantra might not be true.

4. *We avoid and self-soothe with activity.* One of the most common self-soothing techniques for anxious, burned-out executives is to fly into activity. Our default setting is to just keep working—convincing ourselves that staying busy is the answer. Even as the actual results—both at work and home—get worse and worse, we remain addicted to the avoidance technique of working harder and harder. We justify it by saying, "After all, it used to work!"

But the truth is, it is also what led you into burnout—and it will keep you stuck there unless you change your approach.

5. *"It's easier for me to just do it."* I'd be willing to bet you say this more often than you even realize. It's one of the most common phrases we hear from our clients, and it's directly tied to the overachiever traits we've already discussed. As perfectionists who struggle to say no and like to stay busy, the last thing we want to do is delegate. We rationalize it by telling ourselves:

"It's faster and easier if I just do it myself."

But if you've ever said these words—and I'm betting you have—you know what a clever trap they are. The problem with this way of thinking is that it guarantees nothing ever changes. If you continue believing this self-fulfilling prophecy, life can never get better. Instead of making things easier, this mindset inevitably leads to exhaustion. Even worse, when we convince ourselves that it's faster and easier to do everything ourselves, we start to resent the people around us.

We complain that:

- We can't trust our teammates to step up.
- No one else will do the work to our standard.
- Others aren't willing to make the same sacrifices we are.

And so, the burnout cycle continues, fueled by our own refusal to let go.

In the most severe cases, this reluctance—or outright inability—to delegate or loosen the grip of perfectionism, even slightly, can lead to an obsession with work that borders on hoarding. We've seen it firsthand with some of our clients—the work piling up on their desks, unfinished—because they've taken on far too much. And when the inevitable happens—the inability to do it all—the very reputation they've worked so hard to protect starts to crumble.

Paradoxically, the very behaviors meant to ensure success become the thing that leads to failure—to say nothing of the toll on their health, relationships, and overall well-being.

I hope that by recognizing these five common characteristics and the heavy toll they can take, you can see why they can't produce the results you desire. More importantly, I hope it provides the necessary backdrop to make it easier to embrace a new, counterintuitive approach—one that truly works: Goal-Shedding.

This is the game-changer. And as you'll soon see, it's far more effective than simply piling on more goals, more tasks, and more pressure.

Goal-Shedding vs. Goal-Setting

Setting goals is essential for achievement in all areas of life. But for people experiencing burnout, goal-setting can become just another form of addictive avoidance—a way to stay busy rather than truly moving forward. The illusion is that if you set enough goals, you'll somehow control them, and one day, you'll achieve them all. But that day never comes.

I have a client who hoards magazines, believing that one day, she'll finally have time to read them all. She even jokes that as long as she has her piles of unread magazines, she feels like she'll never die!

Now, think of goal-setting in the same way. Just like hoarding magazines, hoarding goals gives the illusion of control—but in reality, it's what got you into burnout in the first place. Instead of liberating you, it traps you in an endless cycle of overcommitment, stress, and exhaustion.

Goal-shedding is a term I use with clients. Instead of setting more goals, it involves *shedding* those that don't align with your values—the values that now drive your new GPS (not your DTEs).

The longer we continue to believe the negative habits and thoughts of our old GPS regarding our goals, the longer we will stay overwhelmed, exhausted, and, paradoxically, unable to do the thing we set out to do: succeed. With your new values-based GPS, you can reset your course to success. Instead of focusing on self-soothing—what I call "giving the bully your lunch money," use your values to make clear-minded choices about what actions will give you the results you want—and set goals from this perspective.

This is the power of goal-*shedding* versus the trap of mere goal-*setting*—prioritizing your actions to fulfill your values instead of chasing your phantom DTEs back into burnout.

At this point in the Burnout Breakthrough System, you have the tools to choose between a new path that leads to a better life and the old habits that keep you stuck in burnout.

GOAL-SHEDDING EXERCISE – Shedding Inventory Category 1: Work

If you're guilty of taking on too much at work and your desk is piled with projects you were afraid to say "no" to, this exercise will help you begin to develop a better habit of dealing with everything that comes your way. If you haven't downloaded the companion PDFs yet for the *Burnout Breakthrough System*, head to the resource section and print out the goal-shedding exercise. Here is what it looks like. When you have your copy, I will walk you through the steps.

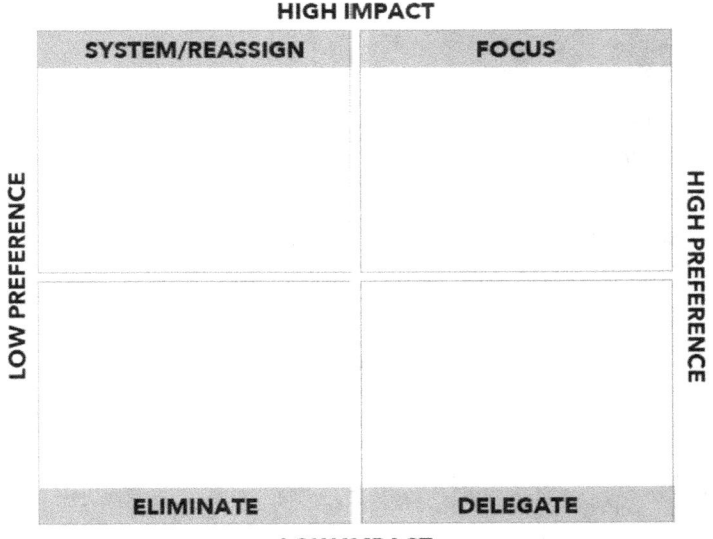

STEP 1: Activity – In the column on the far left labeled "Activity," list those work activities that are top-of-mind and probably giving you grief right now. (You can print multiple copies of this worksheet, depending on how high those stacks on your desk are.)

STEP 2: Better-Faster-Cheaper? – For each activity you listed in the first column, make an assessment. Is there a way that this activity can be done better, faster, or cheaper than by doing it yourself? Based on your assessment, mark this column with either a "Y" for "yes" or a "N" for "no."

STEP 3: Soul Sucking? – Now, do a qualitative assessment of each activity. On a scale of 0 to 5, with 5 being the worst, does doing this activity completely suck the life from your soul? Give each activity the appropriate "soul-sucking" rating.

STEP 4: Only You Can Do It? – This step will force you to ask yourself, "Am I the only one in this whole office that can complete this activity?" If it's true that you're the only one, write a "Y" for "yes" beside each activity in this column. However, if you realize that you're not the only one capable of doing the task, write a "N" for "no."

STEP 5: Shed? – Review your responses in each column to every activity you listed, then based on those responses, decide whether you still want to hang onto it and push harder to complete it, or delegate it to someone else.

I promise you that when you begin to look at your workload pragmatically in this way, you will see that there are other options besides your former default—assuming that it's easier and less hassle for you to do everything yourself. Granted, there will be some activities that only you can do. But it's amazing when I watch clients do this exercise and how quickly they discover that much of what's crowding their desks could be done faster, easier, and cheaper by someone else, giving them back a good deal of their time and, most importantly, their sanity.

Are you surprised by your results—and the tasks you can delegate to someone besides yourself to do it better, faster, and cheaper? How much time did you just earn back—and more importantly, what will you do with that time?

Breaking Through Burnout for Good With Forgiveness

Whenever I think about forgiveness, I remember some advice from one of my most treasured mentors, Click Westin. He used to ask me, "When are you going to be happy?"

For those of us who are terminally goal-oriented, that question sounds ridiculous. When he asked me, I thought the answer was insultingly obvious: "I'll be happy when I achieve all my goals." (Duh.)

Click's response stopped me cold: *"So you're willing to postpone happiness forever?"* I had no answer for that.

In my work with burned-out leaders, CEOs, and executives, I've seen one symptom appear over and over again—and it's one that's even included in the World Health Organization's definition of burnout: Resentment.

I believe resentment is the hidden symptom of burnout. Earlier in this book, we talked about how burnout makes you feel like a victim—trapped by expectations, obligations, and responsibilities. But resentment is one of the most corrosive parts of that victimhood.

It's the slow-burning anger that whispers:

"I give everything to this job, and no one appreciates me."
"Why do I have to do it all?"
"If I don't handle this, everything will fall apart."

And if left unchecked, resentment becomes the fuel that keeps burnout alive.

Before you shut this book and stop reading, I want to say this clearly: most of our clients immediately and vehemently deny feeling like victims, much less admit to having any resentments.

You might be thinking that resentment or forgiveness has nothing to do with your burnout, let alone your recovery. But I encourage you to keep an open mind.

Some of the most powerful moments in my own recovery happened when I faced and released the resentment that was poisoning me. I now know, without a doubt, that letting go of resentment opens the way to forgiveness—and is essential to keeping you from slipping back into burnout. I see this happen with my clients every single day.

Understanding Resentment

Let's be clear about what resentment really is. The word "resentment" literally means "to feel again." Like most other things burned out individuals struggle with, resentment is a self-defeating habit. It traps us in the past, in anger, in frustration—and keeps us running on exhaustion and negativity. You may have heard the old expression: "Resentment is like drinking poison and expecting the other person to die."

Or as my dear friend and mentor, Fr. Tom O'Brien, famously said: "At some point, we have to give up on having a better past."

Facing and releasing resentment through forgiveness— including forgiving yourself—may be the single most important step in your recovery.

I can't emphasize this enough: releasing resentment is the key—

- To break through burnout for good.
- To achieve personal freedom.
- To live a life of joy and fulfillment.

In short, it's the key to never being toast again.

EMBRACE RELEASE TECHNIQUE

Another tool that will help you experience the release of resentment and foster forgiveness for yourself and others is the "ER"—or "Embrace Release technique." I've included a video of the full process in the resources section, but for now, this is a more condensed version of the same technique.

Five Key Steps – Embrace Release Technique

1. *Identify:* List people you resent, starting with the top five. Then, select the one that disturbs you the most. (*Okay, I know—you're going to tell me you don't resent anybody. But really, take a look. Be honest. Nobody has to know but you.*)

2. *Notice:* Close your eyes, breathe deeply, and notice where you feel this resentment in your body—consider its size, shape, color, and temperature. (*Yes, it's similar to practicing the R&R Technique.*) Be patient with yourself if you can't locate the feeling in your body right away. Most people bury their resentments pretty deeply. It can take time to allow them to surface.

3. *Explore:* Reflect on what emotions this energy holds and what it might say if it could speak. (*This is really critical because to release our resentments, we have to give them a voice. Don't worry about what that voice sounds like at this point. Simply allow it to speak.*)

4. *Comfort:* Visualize holding this energy as if you are comforting a crying baby, and allow yourself to comfort it with love and care. *This is counterintuitive. We typically treat our negative energy very unkindly. However, if we allow it to be what it is, we can nurture it into a quiet and peaceful state.*

5. *Release & Reflect:* Take a deep breath to release the energy, journal any lingering thoughts or feelings, and repeat this process whenever resentment arises.

Resentment is a cancer that will eat away at you unless you find a healthy way to release it. Practice the Embrace Release technique until all your crying babies have released that energy and drifted off to sleep.

SENDING LOVE

This technique teaches you to connect with the love you feel for another person and how to transfer it to someone who has been the object of your resentment.

STEP 1: *Focus on Love* – Close your eyes and think of the person you love most.

STEP 2: *Send Love* – Imagine transmitting that love to the person who disturbs you most.

STEP 3: *Amplify Your Love* – Gradually double the amount of love you send, visualizing it growing to 10X, 100X, and even 100,000X.

STEP 4: *Notice Changes* – Continue to send and amplify love and observe any shifts in your feelings or perspective.

STEP 5: *Release and Reflect* – Take a deep breath, release the energy, and journal any lingering thoughts or feelings; repeat as needed.

Like every technique I've shared with you, the more you practice it, the more results you'll see. In this case, with consistent practice, you'll begin to see your resentment transform into forgiveness—bringing you one step closer to breaking free from the isolation that burnout so often creates.

Final Step: Amends

We owe a huge debt of gratitude to our friends in the 12-step programs for providing a clear, powerful, and proven protocol for making amends to those we have harmed. One of the miracles of the 12-step process is that the people we've harmed don't have to accept our amends for the process to work. They don't need to forgive us or even be willing to speak to us again for us to wipe the slate clean and free ourselves from regret and the guilt of resentment.

In my own recovery, I made amends with several coworkers and business partners over time.

- In some cases, it led to mutually healing conversations.
- In others, I wasn't able to repair what had been broken.
- Some people I resented—and tried to make amends with—weren't willing to reconnect.

But here's what mattered most: Regardless of their response, having a genuine desire to take ownership, to fix what I had broken, and to assume 100% responsibility for my actions brought healing in every case—even with those who wanted nothing to do with me.

It would be difficult to improve upon the guidance offered by 12-step programs. In condensed form, this is my understanding of the steps:

MAKING AMENDS: Remember the link to all of these PDFs can be found in the resource section at the end of the book.

STEP 1: *List the People* – Write down a list of names of everyone you believe you have harmed as a result of your burnout.

STEP 2: *List the Harms* – Write specifically what harm you have done to each person. *(Remember, this is about what you did wrong, not them, so keep your side of the street clean and avoid judging others.)*

STEP 3: *Meet-Ups* – Request the opportunity to have a conversation with each person on your list. Have the conversation and ask each person how you can fix what you've broken in the relationship.

STEP 4: *Making Amends* – Based on each person's feedback, fix what you've broken in the relationship to the best of your ability.

STEP 5: *Commit* – Commit to never causing similar harm to this person or anyone else.

(NOTE: The 12-step folks would tell us that the only exception to the process above is when an attempt to make amends might injure that person or others. If you're concerned that might be the case, it's best to consult with a spiritual guide or coach before you proceed.)

I can't say it enough—dealing with your feelings of resentment and making way for forgiveness is not optional. For most people, it is the hardest part of the recovery process but also the one that brings them the greatest relief. It allows you to turn the page on past behaviors so you can fully embrace what's available to you in the next and last breakthrough in the *Burnout Breakthrough System.*

Life Beyond Burnout: What Else Is Possible?

Congratulations! You've made it to the final step in the *Burnout Breakthrough System.*

For me—and for the many people I've worked with—this is where real transformation happens. If you allow the information I've shared to sink in and consistently practice the R&R Technique, along with the other action steps outlined in this chapter, you will experience meaningful change in several ways:

1. *Your energy has returned.* (Most of us feel a new energy that we either haven't felt in a long time—or, more commonly, a level of energy we've never experienced before.)

2. *Your attitude has dramatically changed.* Think back to the Groundhog Day analogy I used at the beginning of the book—where every day felt like an impossibly painful repetition of the one before. Now, that cycle has shifted, and the difference may feel startling.

3. *You feel better*—in your body, your mind, and your spirit—than you have *ever* felt, not just prior to burnout but *ever* in your *life.*

The last step in the Burnout Breakthrough System was born in our earliest face-to-face groups when we asked ourselves a powerful question:

"If we can escape burnout and feel this good, what else is possible in our lives?"

That's exactly what this final step is about—opening the door to what's possible beyond burnout. What else is possible for you? Now that you've broken free from burnout, where can you go next? What new opportunities, relationships, and experiences await you?

This is your moment to step into a life beyond burnout—one driven by purpose, energy, and fulfillment.

What Else Is Possible – Three Goals

GOAL 1: *Locking in your burnout breakthrough*—so you don't slip back into the destructive habits you have broken.

GOAL 2: *Building on the breakthroughs* you've made so far.

GOAL 3: *Taking the next step* "beyond burnout" to your best life ever.

This is where the *Burnout Breakthrough System* really takes wing and flies.

GOAL 1 – Locking in Your Burnout Breakthrough

Nothing is more effective in locking in your recovery from burnout than reviewing your values at the start of each day—and as often as needed throughout.

Think of this as the complement to the mini-vacations from your DTEs that we recommend taking throughout the day. By checking in with your values multiple times, you train yourself to keep them top-of-mind and continually assess your progress in aligning your actions with what truly matters to you.

Over time, this practice becomes automatic. When challenging or disturbing situations arise, instead of falling back into old patterns of reactive, destructive thoughts and behaviors, you will naturally lean on your values—allowing those guiding principles to shape your responses rather than burnout-driven habits.

I am continually amazed by how the behaviors that ruled my life for decades are, for the most part, distant memories. Sometimes, they come to mind when I'm working with clients, but they no longer hold the traction they used to. My old behaviors, if they do bubble to the surface, no longer have a hold on me.

Many of our clients have found it beneficial to stay in contact with other Burnout Breakthrough graduates. (If you would like information about our Beyond Burnout mastermind, or our group and individual coaching programs, or if you have any questions at all, see the link in the resources section.)

GOAL 2 – Building on Your Breakthroughs

I highly recommend that you revisit the three pillars of my *Burnout Breakthrough System* so you maintain momentum and build on your freedom from burnout. At this point, reflect on the goals you have set and consider, with the new energy and positivity you're currently feeling, how you could take those goals even further:

BEYOND BURNOUT—UPPING YOUR GOALS

- What if you set your business goals 10 or 20% higher?
- What if you are able to shed a few goals? Would it be possible for you to work a 20-hour week?
- If so, what would you like to do with that time?
- What if you had the freedom to spend more time with all of the people you love most? How might you spend it?
- What if you had time to engage in philanthropic activities or personal causes that are meaningful to you?

GOAL 3 – What Else Is Possible?

Most graduates of the *Burnout Breakthrough System* notice that as the fog of burnout lifts, their thinking expands to passions and interests they'd never considered before.

This early in your recovery, you might feel like you're walking out of a hospital with your leg in a cast and contemplating a career in tap dancing! But now is the perfect time to expand your thinking—if for no other reason than to not allow it to contract back into the symptomatic, narrow thinking from which you just escaped.

Consider this: If you have broken through burnout for good—*what else is possible?* (Or as the Adidas folks say, "Impossible is Nothing.") Because we focus most of our time on work, let's start your "what else is possible" exploration by stretching your definition of "possible" at work:

WHAT ELSE IS POSSIBLE: WORK-WRITING EXERCISE

STEP 1: *Write your responses to the following questions*:

1. If you had a 200% guaranteed magic wand, what would you wish for in your career?

2. What else could you achieve in your current role?

3. When were you happiest at work, and what made it fulfilling?

4. What do your co-workers or customers say you excel at?

5. Which tasks do you enjoy the most, and how could you do more of them?

6. Which tasks do you enjoy the least, and how could you do less of them?

7. What would your ideal workday and team look like?

8. If you could pursue any career path, what would it be?

STEP 2: *Apply the same questions above to the other important areas of your life*:

- Family
- Friends
- Health & fitness
- Spirituality
- Travel
- Investment
- Giving back

Make sure you access the techniques I have made available in the resources section of the book. I promise you that with consistent practice of the techniques and exercises I've shared:

- The R&R Technique
- The Values Exercise
- Goal-Shedding Exercise
- Embrace Release Technique
- Sending Love Technique
- Making Amends Technique
- What Else Is Possible Exercise

Your burnout will become a distant memory—for good. You will stay free and live the joyful, meaningful, and purposeful life you deserve. In the next chapter, I'll explain the last piece in this freedom from burnout puzzle that is critical for you to stay free and never return.

CHAPTER 8

You're Not in This Thing Alone

Here's the Caveat—You Have to Do the Work.

You can't cherry-pick the steps you like and expect to see results. To achieve freedom from burnout—and, more importantly, stay free—you must commit to every step and consistently practice the techniques.

The steps I've shared may feel counterintuitive, but they are practical and effective. When you boil it all down, burnout is a deeply ingrained habit—one that high achievers often become addicted to. At some point, what once worked—our relentless drive, our perfectionism, our habit of charging harder and running toward the fire—stops working.

That's why you can't treat this book like any other self-help book—reading it once and moving on won't work. There's no way around it: you have to go all in.

I've already stripped the process down to the bare essentials—which means every step matters. You can't skip one. Every technique is rooted in years of experience, and nothing I've included is unnecessary.

There are two things that will guarantee your success:

- Community
- Accountability

Why? Because burnout is the rut of all ruts—its gravitational pull is too strong to escape alone. This work isn't for the faint of heart. It requires fearlessness, commitment, and consistency.

You need a community to pull you out of the isolation of burnout—where relationships begin to fracture and fall away. The ideal scenario is to be surrounded by people who are facing the same challenges and doing the same work.

That's how this all started—six chairs in a basement, sitting in a circle.

We all faced the same struggles.
We understood each other in ways no one else could.
We shared openly.
We held each other accountable—with no BS allowed.

And over time, we watched one another break free from burnout and find lasting freedom. As the group grew, those further along in their recovery inspired the newer members, showing them what was possible on the other side of burnout—if they did the work.

If you're serious about breaking free, you need a community of people who:

- Hold each other accountable for actions and decisions.

- Are committed to doing the same work for the same reasons.
- Want the same results—lasting freedom from burnout.

Your first 90 days of recovery are crucial. This is when you need to see small wins, both in your own progress and in the progress of those around you. Momentum builds courage. Courage builds tenacity. Tenacity leads to transformation.

That's why community is integral to my framework—and the reason I run a mastermind for former high achievers who are ready to stay free from burnout for good. Whether it's my community or another, find one.

You don't have to go at this alone. And I wouldn't recommend that you try. I can't guarantee results if you don't do the work. But I can guarantee that if you commit to every step and practice the techniques consistently, your life will transform—as you step out of the trap of burnout and into lasting freedom.

If you're ready to tackle your number one burnout symptom and get immediate relief, my team and I are here to help. **Schedule a call here: fastfixcall.com.**

Conclusion

As we come to the end of our journey together, my hope is that it's just the beginning for you to begin taking steps toward freedom from burnout. I have shared everything you need—you just need to decide to take action.

In this final chapter, I want to return to the theme of hope and remind you of the most essential ideas to your recovery—so you can live in complete confidence that your burnout is gone for good.

1. **There is hope.** When I began this work, I was the biggest skeptic of all. My life felt completely hopeless. But I've recovered completely and I'm living my best life ever—better than my best day pre-burnout. This is true for executives and leaders across the country and around the globe who have followed the program and done the work. You can, too. In fact, I guarantee it.

2. **You are causing your own burnout.** Don't let that truth discourage you. This is good news! If you can cause it, then you can fix it. You don't have to wait for your colleagues or customers to change. The power to change and recover lies within you.

3. **You can recover quickly.** Your recovery from burnout doesn't have to take months or years. In fact, you can fully recover in 90 days or less (and for good) if you

follow the simple techniques I have shared in this book.

4. **You can't control your thoughts and emotions—and you don't have to.** Despite what you may believe or may have been taught over your lifetime, controlling your thoughts and emotions is not necessary to be comfortable in your own skin and successful in your career. You don't have to control your brain any more than you have to control your gallbladder or any other organ. You just have to let go. Remember, you are not your thoughts.

5. **Your energy is the first thing that will return.** Contrary to your cultural conditioning, you'll get your energy back not by taking a long weekend, a vacation, or a sabbatical. You can accomplish more in five seconds toward recovering your energy (using the R&R Technique) than you could with five days or weeks of time off.

6. **Your confidence will return.** As you regain your energy, you'll find your confidence comes back with it. The root of that newfound confidence is the knowledge that your disturbing thoughts and emotions can no longer bully you.

7. **Clarity and optimism will replace being overwhelmed and depressed.** When you commit to your values as your new GPS, they will lead to fulfillment in every area of your life.

8. **You will experience a life beyond burnout that is better than any of your best days pre-burnout.** You'll discover a new life beyond exhaustion to enjoy genuine joy and satisfaction.

You now have everything you need to break through burnout in 90 days or less and put it behind you forever. But if you need help along the way and want to join a community of like-minded leaders discovering life beyond burnout, we would be happy to help.

To see how my team and I work, I want to offer you a free call to get some immediate relief from your number one burnout symptom. Schedule a call here, you won't regret it: fastfixcall.com

I want to leave you with these final thoughts: Believe that there is a way out of burnout. Believe that this is the guidebook that will get you on your way. Mostly, believe that you're not toast.

Resources

Burnout Assessment: https://form.jotform. com/203086520756152

This assessment will pinpoint the exact symptoms that burnout is causing in your life as well as help you identify the severity of your burnout.

Beyond Burnout Values Assessment Exercise: https:// tinyurl.com/495dsvsh

After you have completed the Values Assessment, I highly recommend scheduling a call with one of our skilled coaches as a 2nd step. They can help you interpret the results of your values assessment and begin to create your own burnout recovery blueprint. The call is free of charge—our gift to you to help get you on the road to a permanent recovery.

Goal-Shedding Exercise – https://doubledareyou.us/ wp-content/uploads/2025/01/Module_7_Goal-Shedding_ Worksheet_1_-_Task_Evaluation.pdf

Embrace/Release Technique Video – https://vimeo. com/1044432551/f5e9d704fd

Making Amends Video – https://vimeo.com/1044432966/ e31de7319c

Making Amends Worksheet – https://doubledareyou. us/wp-content/uploads/2025/01/Module-8-Amends-Worksheet.pdf

For information on our Beyond Burnout mastermind group or our group and individual coaching programs, please email us at info@BurnoutBreakthrough.com.

In addition to the *Burnout Breakthrough* PDFs, I want to share the work of a few incredibly bright people whose visionary work helped me to craft this successful Burnout Breakthrough System. Each book was a revelation to me and provided enormous inspiration for how this framework was designed:

> *The Untethered Soul,* by **Michael Singer** – A seminal book about what lives inside you and how to liberate yourself by developing a positive consciousness.

> *The Happiness Trap,* by **Russ Harris, MD** – Harris offers practical applications of Acceptance and Commitment Therapy (ACT) for dealing with stress and worry, building better relationships, and finding more fulfillment in life.

> *Get Out of Your Mind and Into Your Life,* by **Stephen C. Hayes, PhD** – Another great book based on ACT techniques for letting go of pain, assessing your values and letting those values guide and motivate you.

The Book of Forgiving: The Fourfold Path for Healing Ourselves and Our World, by **Desmond Tutu** – A profound book by a Nobel laureate on the four-step process of forgiveness and that granting it and receiving it is the greatest gift to humankind.

About the Author

Scott Anderson is a serial entrepreneur, executive coach, and licensed mental health therapist who is passionate about helping high-achieving professionals break free from burnout and build businesses that truly thrive—without sacrificing their personal lives.

With over 35 years of experience, having successfully launched 10 businesses and sold eight (with the scars to prove it—as Scott says), he knows the pressures of leadership intimately. His unique blend of business insight and therapeutic expertise has earned him recognition in Forbes and Entrepreneur magazines.

What really sets Scott apart is his genuine heart for helping others succeed while finding balance and joy. His coaching has empowered hundreds of CEOs and entrepreneurs to work smarter, reclaim their time, and reignite their passion for both work and life.

Outside of work, you'll find Scott going for walks with his wife or enjoying the antics of Phyllis, his lovable English bulldog "assistant," who is always ready to lend her expertise to the situation.

Scott's latest book is packed with real, actionable strategies to help move you forward while stressing less and rediscovering the joy in your journey.